Trading for a bright future

TRADING BELIEFS for TRADING PROFITS

by

Martin Cole

Trading for a bright future

Trading for a Bright Future by Martin Cole

Copyright Martin Cole 2001

Martin Cole asserts the moral right to be identified as the author of this work.

First Print 2001

First published in Great Britain by:
Home Gate Publications
68 Tenter Road
Moulton Park
Northampton NN3 6AX

ISBN 0-9540483-0-X

Cover design Martin Cole and Ryan Lambie

Printed by Candor Print, Northampton

Visit Martin Cole's website: www.learningtotrade.com

All rights reserved. No part of this book shall be reproduced, stored in a retrieval system, or transmitted by any means, electronic, mechanical, photocopying, recording, or otherwise, without written permission from the publisher. No patent liability is assumed with the respect to the use of the information contained herein. Although every precaution has been take in the preparation of this book, the publisher and the author assume no responsibility for errors or omissions. Neither is any liability assumed for damages resulting from the use of the information contained herein.

For Denise

My wife, my best friend and mother of our two wonderful adventurous sons. Having you by my side always makes me feel like the richest man on the planet.

Trading for a bright future

TABLE OF CONTENTS

Dedication		3
Author's Preface		6
Preface		7
Chapter One	Why all the excitement about trading?	9
Chapter Two	My Journey	13
Chapter Three	Understanding the Market	19
Chapter Four	The Market and the People who Work it	27
Chapter Five	What is being bought and sold	39
Chapter Six	Becoming a Trader; Important Considerations	49
Chapter Seven	Managing your Personal Circumstances	73
Chapter Eight	Getting down to Business	89
Chapter Nine	Introducing the Bright Futures Strategy	105
Chapter Ten	A Deeper Understanding of Market Trends	131
Chapter Eleven	The Psychology of Decision Making	145
Chapter Twelve	The Curse of the Lollipop	157
Chapter Thirteen	The Wrap-up	165
Glossary		169

Trading for a bright future

AUTHOR'S PREFACE

The inspiration behind writing this book was my desire to contribute something to the 'common man', in other words, to people like myself.

All of us need a helping hand from time to time. I was fortunate enough to be literally lifted onto the first rung of the ladder of my success by a close friend, Brian Loughran. Back in 1995, I mentioned that I was thinking of opening a pizza delivery business. Brian knew that I did not have a great deal of money, but he agreed to let me rent his premises, without a written lease and took no up-front payment. He even helped with the conversion of the building, refusing to accept anything for all his hard work. *"It will all come right in the end"* became his catchcry.

Just under two years later, my wife and I sold the business as a going concern. Apart from a handshake with Brian, I had no legal agreement to sell the lease, but I was lucky enough to keep the full proceeds from the sale, while Brian gained from the increased value to his property. Indeed it had come right in the end, for both of us.

Brian's handshake ultimately made it possible for us to enter the trading environment and move to Spain. Thank you, Brian.

I hope that this book proves to be the helping hand that eases you, the reader, onto the first rung of the ladder of your own success, and that *it will all come right in the end* for you too.

Trading for a bright future

PREFACE

I first met Martin on the phone in early 1997 when he came to me to buy a datafeed. At once, I knew this was no ordinary customer. I immediately sensed the gravity of the man - the passion, avid intent and immense will to succeed.

Martin has won the battle that many fight with trading. But the battle has made him, unlike many, want to take others with him over the hills and mountains to victory. As people who have traded know - and those who have not are yet to find out - the journey through the markets is as much a personal one as one of having to implement this or that trading technique. Martin's training in psychology has helped and continues to help traders. His vision gives perspective to what can otherwise be confusing terrain to navigate.

When I met Martin, my personal trading had come to a halt. After a brief description of the problem I was having he gave me some advice. The next day I traded using that advice, and made five winning intra day trades in rapid succession. Martin had "popped a lollipop"[1], as he puts it. A blockage had existed in my mind and he simply helped me see and expunge it.

In his courses and in this book, Martin will, I am sure, continue to hold the hands of many traders all the way to success. His record speaks for itself. The self-effacing, dry Northamptonshire exterior he projects hides a man of immense gravitas, sensitivity and extreme intelligence, combined with a common, decent touch that makes for a rare combination.

I believe that through his book and courses Martin will continue to help many traders on their path to success and self realisation through their trading. If you have the courage to seek the truth, Mr Cole can help you realise your worthwhile ambitions in the markets.

Martin, on behalf of many of us, past and present, whom you have helped and continue to assist - a big "Thank you" from us all. We wish you every success.

Larry Levy

---

[1] *See chapter twelve for an explanation of this colourful metaphor.*

Trading for a bright future

CHAPTER ONE

Why all the excitement about trading?

Trading - the exchange of goods between individual people or institutions - is as old as human society itself, and today it exists among all organised groups of people, from the most complex, technological societies to small-scale groups still living in the Stone Age, even if the goods that are traded are very different.

The exchange of valued items has been the impetus behind every imperialistic movement, irrespective of ethnicity. European societies (including the British, the Spanish and the Dutch) colonised Africa, the Americas, parts of Asia and elsewhere in order to have access to goods with which to trade and accumulate wealth. All around the world, peoples from the Aztec to the Zulu have developed social relations, conquered and been defeated to further commercial interests.

The history of human existence is, to a very large extent, *the history of trading*. The question of access to material goods has been behind most alliances and as many wars, has been the reason for strategic marriages between important families, and the inspiration of many religious practices. It is part of what we are. Even though the hunter-gatherer's exchange of a bow and arrow for another useful item may seem to be very different to the buying and

Trading for a bright future

selling in a modern marketplace, the impulses behind the deal are very much the same.

The modern trader must never forget that the qualities of 'use' and 'value' are very subjective. If a social group (or an individual person) *believes* that an object is valuable, then, effectively, it *is*. The belief in use or value of an object is the impetus behind the sale [2], rather than that objects actual value - if indeed 'actual value' can even be said to exist at all.

Modern trading is a complex, multi-national business, involving individuals and large corporations who work with cutting-edge technology and with their most important tools - their intelligence and understanding of the market. In its contemporary form, trading remains the driving force behind national and international movements. To an immeasurable extent, the failure or success of governments and alliances is determined by important actors in the trading sphere. Now, thanks to the increasing accessibility of technology, and the fact that trading is conducted more and more on the Internet, it is possible for many people from different walks of life and educational backgrounds to enter the market as independent traders.

People sometimes ask "what type of person becomes a trader?" - and to that there is no straight-forward answer. There is not a simple 'traders personality', there are simply prepared and unprepared traders, weak and strong players in the market.

This book is for two groups of people - those who have never traded, and wish to start off on the right foot, and

---

[2] The vast medieval trade in religious items such as bones purported to be of Jesus Christ is an excellent example of the dominion of subjective belief over objectivity in assessing an items value.

Trading for a bright future

those who already experimented with trading, with less than satisfactory results.

Many books about the market and trading concentrate on the 'how-to' elements of the business. Here, we will be examining not only the basics of the market and trading, but also a frequently neglected element that is at least as important; the impact that your personality, your subconscious and the people around you have on your trading performance. People are not machines, but emotive beings – not a bad thing in itself, but certainly a factor that has to be monitored and controlled in an environment that makes no allowances for a bad day. Awareness of one's potential strengths and weaknesses is the first - and most important - step in launching oneself upon the market. It is my intention to help you to know yourself better and, in doing so, to become a successful trader. My aim in creating this book is to bring to you the advice that I wish I'd had at hand when I started trading, and to help you to avoid the mistakes I made. This book is a forum for the introduction of my 'Bright Futures' trading strategy - a trading system that has succeeded, not only for me, but also for those with whom I have shared it.

Any new enterprise brings with it a new vocabulary, so don't be surprised if you find quite a few unfamiliar words in the text. A glossary has been provided at the back of the book for easy reference. My advice is to have a quick look at the glossary before beginning, and then to use it whenever you encounter a word you are not entirely certain of. As the world of trading is opened before you, you will find that using terms that may have confused you at first will quickly become second nature.

The most important attitude to bring to any new

enterprise is optimism, mixed with just the right amount of humility and willingness to learn. Approach trading with an open mind, and be ready to challenge, not only your conception of what trading is all about, but also your preconceptions about yourself. You may find that both are rather different than you thought.

CHAPTER TWO

My Journey

My name is Martin Cole. I am a trader and, more importantly, a husband and father of a family. Today, I enjoy a comfortable lifestyle in the south of Spain, but I wasn't born into a life of privilege. For me, the road to prosperity has been a long and winding one.

The third of six children, I grew up on a small farm in the village of Towcester in Northamptonshire, England. Our father, Jim, hoped that we would all become farmers, but although it took me many years to find my professional path, I always knew that agriculture was not for me. While never a very academic child, I was bright. "He can turn his hand to anything" was the comment people used to make, and I have certainly turned my hand to plenty of activities over the years. While I didn't discover for a long time that my strength lay in trading, I always felt that I was destined to do something unusual with my life, and that I was capable of much more than I seemed to be achieving.

I met my lovely wife when she was just sixteen and a half and I almost as young, and I knew straight away that she was the one for me. She didn't realise so quickly, though, and stood me up three times before we finally went out on our first date! We got married when we were eighteen and twenty. Denise has supported me in everything I have done, through difficult times, bankruptcy, success and everything in between. Her philosophy has always been: *'Just do it. If you don't, you might regret it.'* We have two wonderful sons and Denise is even more beautiful now than she was all those years ago. Even if I had not managed to make trading succeed for me, having her would have made me a very lucky man.

My interest in psychology began when I was working in sales in my late twenties. I felt that if I understood peoples' thought processes more that I would be better able to manipulate them and improve my sales! Not a great approach, but years later my studies bore fruit in a way that I had never anticipated. At that time, I simply began reading every self-help book that I could get my hands on. As the years passed, my interest in human behaviour gradually grew until I reached the stage where I felt I needed some formal training, so I enrolled on a hypnotherapy course in Regent's college in London.

I did work in hypnotherapy for some time - helping people to quit smoking, overcome their phobias and so on - but although the work was interesting and rewarding, I still had not found my niche. I returned to business and became involved in the building industry, meeting with some success until the British economy collapsed, along with my order book. In that year 1990, there was a 75 per cent increase in bankruptcies in the area where we lived. We lost everything, our house, our lifestyle - the lot - and were left with no choice but to return with our two small boys, Steven and James, to live in a mobile home at my parents' place in Towcester, Northamptonshire. I went to work with my father and Denise took a range of menial jobs, cleaning and so on, just to make ends meet.

Trading for a bright future

Between us and with the help of a close friend, we saved up enough money to open a business, a pizza restaurant. We kept on our day jobs, and worked in the restaurant at night. Those were difficult times. Our sons were little more than babies, and we would put them to sleep upstairs in the restaurant and take them home, still sleeping, at one or two in the morning before getting up again to start another day. The pressure that the situation put on our little family was horrendous. We kept going for fourteen months until we managed to sell the business and make a small profit. At that stage we really needed a break from everything so we headed off to Greece, with the idea that we might be able to find something to do there. We didn't.

Greece is a beautiful country, but without an occupation I ended up sitting in front of our rented house doing nothing but contemplate the view and my rapidly increasing waistline! After about three months we realised that we were not doing the right thing, and we headed back to England, harsh reality, hard work, and a new house. Business had its ups and downs, and then, at last, I got interested in trading. The spark was finally ignited by a copper trading scandal that was making waves. Coincidentally, at around the same time I got an unsolicited mailing in the post, advertising a trading course. Something clicked in my mind and I felt sure that this could be a good way to escape all the hassles and problems of a traditional business. I spent a couple of months trying to work out how to do it, paper trading, holding positions over night, and just trying to get a handle on the business, but without letting any real money get involved. At this stage, I knew absolutely nothing about the technical side of trading, I had never even seen a live chart on a screen, and so I worked exclusively from newspapers until I realised that what I was doing was not practical in terms of trying to make a living. I still needed more information.

My first contacts told me about data feeds and other technical details, but I wasn't informed enough to know exactly what I needed. Eventually, I got in touch with a broker in London. He asked me what I knew about marketing, and suggested that I get in touch with a gentleman who was offering training in trading and I completed a course with him over a number of weekends. As it happens, we were largely taught theoretical information with little practical use, but as I had no reference point with which to judge, I wasn't aware of the courses discrepancies. Nonetheless, the course introduced me to the world of trading and for that reason, I have no regrets for having taken it.

After completing the course, I decided to sell the business in which I was involved, making a profit of twelve thousand pounds, which I invested in a data feed, software and a broker's account. In the first six weeks, I made six and a half thousand pounds profit, and really thought that I'd found Utopia! It was incredible. Reality struck pretty quickly, however, and soon I found myself just holding my own. Losing a little, winning a little. Things seemed to be going horribly wrong, and my stress levels were affecting not just me, but also my wife and children. I reached the point where I felt that everything was against me. The market was against me. The world was against me. No matter what I did, I lost – to the extent of carrying out thirty-two losing trades in succession! That was my turning point. At that moment, my training in psychology came to the fore and I recognised that the failures were being generated by myself. My own subconscious was trying to remove me from a stressful area by bankrupting me, leaving me with no choice but to leave the market - *I believed that I was going to lose and my belief became self-fulfilling.* I stopped trading, and spent three or four months analysing myself and other peoples' trading practices, becoming fascinated by the way peoples' beliefs affect the market and themselves. Whereas before I had visualised the market as a sort of free-standing entity, I now saw it as a sea of people, rather than prices. A sea of indecision and fear. So many people just didn't know what they were doing and were, essentially, gambling.

I decided to apply what I knew about psychology to understand the way peoples' belief structures are manifested in the market. I was able to map the market in terms of belief structures, and this clarity of vision enabled me to lose my own trepidation. I started trading again, and now there were no gambles, just steady earning. Gains were held, and losses minimised quickly. I was also trading much less than I had done before, just once or twice a day, and sometimes as little as once or twice a week. As my account grew, so did my confidence.

Then, destiny stepped in the form of Alex Whitcombe, a computer expert I contacted for help with some technical issues. When he opened my machine, he recognised that it had trading equipment installed, and we started to talk. Although he had done a little trading, he wasn't involved in it at that moment, but he did want to be free from business. As our friendship developed, Alex would come and watch me trade, and eventually he gave up his business and got into the market himself.

At this stage I approached him with a proposal.

Trading for a bright future

I wanted to get my ideas about using belief structures to trade turned into a software programme. I carried on trading, and he started to develop his programming skills. As his expertise grew, we worked together creating software packages for mapping the market - none of which were successful in the long-term, but we were getting close. I started looking at belief structures as they were manifested within a single day's trading, trying to identify the days when it seemed likely that I was going to lose money, so as to avoid trading during those times. My success in identifying 'no-trade' days did wonders for my account. I was trading less and earning more. At last Denise and I were free to think about leaving England. We decided to sell up and go to Spain. Our house went for a profit, and so we headed for the sun. I continued working with Alex, and between us we produced a piece of software which we called 'Bright Futures', a very simple piece of end-of-day software. A financial journalist investigated the program and found that it worked eight times out of ten, an extraordinary success in terms of trading software.[3]

My family and I have been living in Spain for three years now. The boys go to school in Competa, and speak Spanish like natives! Our families often come and visit, and although I wouldn't even start trying to explain trading to our parents, I know that they're happy for us.

I am blissfully happy with my life, my family, my wife and my career. Everything has worked out perfectly. I am still trading, and occasionally offer courses in live trading here in Competa, Southern Spain. Perhaps I'll see you here some day.

[3] Webb, Andrew, *Beyond Belief*, FOW Intermarket Intelligence for the Risk Professional, Issue 343, December 1999, pp. 22-4.

CHAPTER THREE

Understanding the Market

Although the exchange of goods is as old as time, the market in its modern form is a relatively recent phenomenon, dating from the latter half of the nineteenth century. The recent explosion in technological advancement has brought about tremendous changes, making trading accessible to a much wider range of people than ever before, and even democratising the process to a large extent.

There are two principal types of markets, the *cash* or *spot markets*, and the *futures'* or *forward markets*, both of which can be traded using the Bright Futures strategy which will be explained in detail in chapter nine. The 'cash market' in equities, for example, is the stock market as we know it for buying and selling shares. The 'futures' market is a speculative future value of an index such as the Dow Jones, DAX or FTSE 100, on which one can speculate by buying or selling the speculative 'future' value on 'margin' - for instance, ten percent of the real value of the instrument. The margin allows the trader to 'gear' his account, so that he can trade in a future on a share for a value of, for example 10 pence for an actual move in the share of one. This clearly opens up possibilities for high profit or loss gearing, and therefore increased risk. This book will help identify lower risk opportunities for that higher gearing, and explain how to limit your losses when things do not work out as planned - so that you may return to trade again.

If you are to become a trader, you will need to be clear about the differences between the types of market, so we'll start by setting the record straight.

The **cash market** is, quite simply, a forum for the exchange of goods as diverse as gold, agricultural products, and computer parts. Items are bought and sold. Depending on the commodities in question, payments are made in actual cash or in cash instruments.

The **futures market** seems much more abstract at first glance. Essentially, the traders buy and sell goods which are not immediately available, but which will become so at a specific future date, with a traded price. Let's examine these markets in some more detail.

Cash Markets

Market makers are the most important force behind movements in equity cash markets.[4] In order to understand what the cash market is, and how it operates, it is vital that you acquire a full understanding of the part they play - both their real one, and the perceived one - which are, as you will see, much more different than most people imagine. A failure to understand, or a partial understanding of what they do is behind many, if not most, trading failures. You owe it to yourself to invest a little time and patience acquiring some important information *before* you begin to trade.

[4] While this is generally true of the stock market, it may not *always* be so of the commodities cash market.

Trading for a bright future

In the case of equities, if the market makers are holding for instance, 1000 shares of XYZ, and a demand for that stock begins to develop, they will mark it up in value, in order to make as large a profit as possible. Let's suppose that, while the demand lasts, 100 shares of XYZ were sold, leaving the market maker with 100 lots, now marked up to the new price. The remaining set of 900 is probably now worth more than the initial 1000. As this scenario is repeated over and over again, it generates a higher and higher price for the outside buyer and an increasing stock value for the market maker. During this time, the market maker must make a bid price (the price at which he buys the stock), which rises in tandem with the increasing ask price (the price at which stock is sold off to the customer).[5]

While all of this is going on, traders are observing the market and making decisions about what to buy and sell. Many do not focus their attention to a sufficient degree on the actions the market maker is taking and, more importantly, exactly *why* he is taking them. These traders do not make fully informed trading decisions, and are unlikely to remain in a winning position for very long. So that you will never join their ranks I will be placing a great deal of emphasis on the role of the market maker in the chapters that follow, and on the vantage point that the Bright Futures Strategy enables you to have.

Futures or Forward Markets

The concept of trading in an environment where goods do not really exchange hands is initially challenging. To make

---

[5] The bid price sometimes lags behind farther than normal in a very fast-moving market.

the idea of futures trading more accessible, let's take a brief look at the origins of the idea.

Futures trading came into being as a way to deal with the seasonal nature of many important products, especially perishable goods. Merchants dealing in perishable products gradually evolved a type of futures trading by issuing receipts that entitled the bearer to a certain quantity of the product when it became available. Holders of the receipts could then exchange them, and the receipts themselves acquired a certain value. Such were its beginnings. Modern futures markets came into being in order to guarantee a future price. In the case of agricultural products, the future price of delivery can be guaranteed by selling the crop at the market price before it is available. This has obvious advantages for the producer, and also guarantees the buyer that he will be able to obtain the product at a certain price in the market.

While over the years the range of products involved has widened and changed, the essence of future trading remains the same. Traders deal with contracts that require the delivery of the product in question at a certain date in the future, at a specified price. Rather than trading in goods, they trade in the *promise of future goods.* However, in recent years, the introduction of modern futures markets (such as the German/Swiss Eurex all electronic market) have led to faster market movement and much more open access for the individual, who can now trade in seconds from a terminal anywhere in the world.

In the futures market, the traders are the most important actors, fulfilling the useful function of keeping the market mobile. Here there are no market makers as such, just big traders. They set bid and ask prices for their own accounts or on behalf of someone else. Traders working for their own accounts are known as 'local' traders, while others are employed by large brokers and banks, which usually pay them a salary and prohibit them from trading for their own account.

The key thing to remember in futures trading is that the majority of traders are 'speculative' - in other words they do not intend to take delivery of the shares in an index or oil in a commodity futures, but are trading on a 'geared margined' basis for high profits from relatively short term movements. Because of the high gearing, profit and loss fluctuations may be greater in futures trading than in other types of investment activity.

What does the stock market offer a company ?

Markets offer companies the possibility of raising capital by selling stock to outside investors. The very first time a company offers stock to the public, it is sold at a standard, non-fluctuating price, known as the 'initial public offering'. At this stage, shares are generally sold without the intervention of the stockbroker. The price is referred to as the 'opening price'. Now that the company has been made public, shares can be sold in the market in the usual way and if everything goes well for the company and its investors, values will rise and everyone will make a profit.

Trading for a bright future

•

To sum up, the basic difference between the cash and the futures market is that in a stock exchange, as an example of a cash market, the stocks bought and sold represent partial ownership in the company which originally made the stock available.

A cash market is for immediate exchange and a futures market represents the exchange of a commodity or a determined number or value of an index at a predetermined date in the future. In reality, the cash market needs to have transactions settled in full almost immediately. In the case of the futures market one can actually trade the value of the future contract on a geared basis, thus trading on price differences. This appeals to the person who wishes to trade in and out for a few points.

There is often a defined mathematical relationship between a cash and a futures market which maintains a certain price differential. In turbulent times stock index futures may trade at a discount to the cash market, which is expected to fall imminently, and are following the futures down. In general, the stock futures market will trade at a small calculated premium to the cash stock market, which will fall steadily on a calculated basis until expiry day, when it will be traded at exactly the level of the cash market.

In a futures exchange, *contracts* are bought and sold. These are standardised as to quality, quantity, delivery time and location, so as to enable a common tradable unit for future delivery. The quality that changes is that of price, which is revealed through trading. The contracts represent the intent to accept or deliver a quantity of a product at some future date.

Trading for a bright future

Subsequent chapters examine in detail the roles of important players in the market, and explain how you can apply your understanding of how the market works to becoming a successful trader.

Trading for a bright future

CHAPTER FOUR

The Market and the People who Work it

Of course, it is not possible to discuss all the markets in the world, or even a large percentage of them in this book, but we can scratch the surface by examining the profiles of a number of famous markets, both electronic and those which are still housed in physical locations, such as the New York Stock Exchange (also known as Wall Street).[6]

If you have some interest in the market and trading, and as you are reading this book, one supposes that you do, you will already be familiar with the names of the most important international markets. Even the least trading-conscious person cannot help but encounter financial news in his or her daily life. All of us feel the consequences of trading action in one way or another, whether in the changing value of our country's currency or that of the stocks and shares we hold.

While a few major markets still have trading floors, most trading is now conducted in the electronic realm, and those working in the market will often deal with many people whom they never physically meet, probably making the world-wide community of traders the largest virtual community that exists.

---

[6] Even the New York Exchange is partly electronic, thanks to its Superdot system which is used for small order execution.

Trading for a bright future

The following are just a few of the many markets around the world, although it is fair to say that they are certainly among the most important, with a large percentage of the globe's trading money passing through them. All maintain informative, accessible websites, and it is very much worth your while browsing through them. Each trader must choose the market or markets that suit him best, and considerable research is necessary.

SOME IMPORTANT MARKETS

The London Stock Exchange

This is Britain's leading stock exchange, and also one of the most international of all exchanges. It provides investors with the opportunity to buy and sell shares in the British or international companies that interest them, thus enabling the companies in question to raise money. The market has a venerable history, tracing its origins to the seventeenth century. Since 1986, it has been in the electronic domain rather than on the trading floor.

The exchange maintains a variety of markets tailored to the needs of different kinds of companies. Most British and international shares are listed in the main market, while the Alternative Investment Market offers space to developing companies. Technology companies are represented by techMARK, within the principal market.

The New York Stock Exchange

The New York Stock exchange, with two hundred years of trading under its belt, still operates a trading floor where

Trading for a bright future

exchange members do substantial business for their investors using the old-fashioned method, while small orders are carried out by the system's small order execution system, known as Superdot, which trades both national and international equities. American companies still represent a large majority, although international companies are increasingly represented.

The market shares an electronic trading system with other U.S. markets which traders can access by computer. Larger orders are still handled manually via the physical floor. Traders who want to do business here need to place an order with their broker, who must be a member of the exchange, and in the case of smaller orders he or she can now execute through their broker via the Internet, instantly.

NASDAQ

No doubt you have heard the name NASDAQ mentioned in the news, even if you have never traded before. NASDAQ has seen spectacular growth in recent years. The market, which was founded in 1971 as the world's first electronic stock market, is controlled from the United States. NASDAQ exists mainly in the electronic domain, broadcasting information simultaneously to over half a million computer terminals around the world. Traders use the information to decide what they are going to buy and sell and will often execute their orders electronically.

FOREX

The FOREX market developed in the 1970s when floating

exchange rates were re-established as a cash inter-bank or inter-dealer market. The most important foreign exchange activity is the business between the dollar and the four major currencies (British Pound, Eurodollar, Swiss Franc, and Japanese Yen.) There is no centralised trading area; trading occurs over the telephone and through computer terminals.

DAX

The XETRA DAX or *Deutsche Atkienindex,* which was introduced in 1988, is the leading German stock index. At the time of its introduction, the DAX was the only representative of what in subsequent years became a family of stock market indexes in Germany. The DAX was the first performance index ever to serve as an underlying for derivatives trading. This futures market is entirely electronic. The XETRA DAX Future is traded on the combined German/Swiss futures market, known as Eurex. Because I largely trade the DAX, many of the illustrations I use, especially in explaining the Bright Futures Strategy, are based on it. However, the points I make are equally applicable to other markets.

Important People in the Trading Arena; the Cast

The market is a place where futures are made, hearts are broken, and adrenaline is the drug of choice for many. In trading, you are entirely alone, at once your own best friend and worst enemy. All other traders, while they have nothing against you personally, want to win, and every time somebody wins, another person loses.

Trading for a bright future

As in the case of any great drama, the chief instigators of the plot are not always who they seem to be. This latter fact is overlooked by many traders, but it is very important to recognise its truth if you intend to make regular profits while trading, and to realise that apparently random market behaviour is frequently carefully executed from behind the scenes, with the aim of influencing the bulk of traders. The market's inner mechanisms are every bit as complex as the most convoluted of Shakespearean plots, pivotal characters are not always what they seem, and one person can play more than one role at the same time. The market is even more exciting than fiction because the results of market activity infiltrate every aspect of daily life. Let's take a look at the main players and examine what they do.

The Market Maker

A market maker[7] is a firm that is attached to the stock exchange, engaging in the buying and selling of stocks, shares, bonds, and so on. The actions it performs establish a market for these securities.

In recent decades, many market makers have also taken over the role of jobber, or principal buyer and seller of securities, as well the role of stockbroker, acting as an agent for the buyers and sellers. There are still some firms

---

[7] In the text, I will refer to 'market makers' as though they were individual persons for the sake of clear prose. You must appreciate, however, that a market maker is usually an institution comprised of individuals rather than a single person *per se*. In the text, I refer to many actors in trading as 'he'. In this choice of terminology I do not wish to suggest in any way that trading is a masculine activity - it reflects the limitations of the English language rather than a male bias.

that specialise solely in stock broking - the execution of the purchases and sales made by traders.

The market making firm derives part of its profit from the difference of the price at which it buys the stock - the bid price - and the price at which it sells it - the ask price. Market makers also sometimes run a stock higher (mark prices up) and attempt to sell stock if they expect lower prices, and they will also mark prices lower in expectation of a rise. They are in a unique position to play the market. Markets are constantly mobile, and supply and demand never cease to ebb and flow. Market makers are constantly marking prices up and down, in relation to their holdings of the security that is rising or falling in quality. They are experts at manipulating the fears - and hence behaviour - of the vast sea of amateur traders who do not even realise that they are being controlled from behind the scenes.

There are a number of types of market makers. The retail market-making firm has a brokerage network serving individual investors. It provides them with a continuous flow of orders or sales opportunities, ensuring stability in the marketplace and ease of movement for the company's stock.

The institutional market-making firms make large block orders for such institutions as mutual funds, pensions funds, insurance companies, and asset management companies.

Regional market-making firms deal with investors and companies of a particular region, providing detailed information about that area.

Wholesale market-making firms have institutional clients for whom they trade shares, and also deal with broker-dealers who are not registered as market makers in a company's stock. They are a very important source of shares for retail, institutional and regional firms.

You must *never forget* that the market maker is in an extremely powerful position, which he maintains through his overview of the market in terms of its strengths and weaknesses. He is able to monitor supply and demand, and knows in advance when large blocks of buying or selling are going to come into the market.

While the market maker tends not to flaunt himself, his presence infiltrates every marketing scene, and he manipulates the fears of amateur traders, thus determining their actions to a large extent. Financial journalists frequently consult market markers or city spokesmen for their interpretations of the market, and in this way, the news can be very reflective of their stance, rather than of objective reality.

If you hope to become a successful trader, one of your most important tasks will be to learn how to think as he does, and to anticipate market reactions to his actions.

The Press

The press tends to present itself as impartial and objective, but in terms of financial news, it is often the market maker's right hand, packaging manipulation as information, and leading the masses to exactly where he wants them. Learn to distrust financial news, or at least to receive every item with a healthy dose of scepticism, because what the papers report is often only partly true. Market makers have access to the media, and every reason to wish to control the movements of the traders. The financial news reported in all major newspapers never reflects the whole truth of underlying market activity. It reveals the value of securities and illustrates trends but does not show the reason for the values, or the fact that prices may be forced down or up depending on what the market maker wants the bulk of traders to do.

'Amateur Traders', Weak Holders

These are volatile players in the market whose moods can swing from excitement to despair during astonishingly brief periods of time. While amateurs may feel themselves to be in control of the situation, in fact they are often psychologically controlled by the market makers, who lead them in such a way as to serve their own purposes.

Weak holders are those that have probably purchased stocks on the basis of media hype at the time of flotation. Their understanding of the market is limited. They listen to outside information services and pay attention to the financial press. They have limited funds with which to trade and are often over-extended in terms of investment portfolio. They, being interested in quick results and easy profits, consider this to be an acceptable risk. All too often, these are traders that are forced to leave the market as they are unable to sustain a viable position.

Amateurs or weak holders can make profits in the short term but they are unlikely to be able to maintain a winning position for very long. Sadly, they represent the majority of traders and are responsible for the common perception of trading as glorified gambling.

Well-Prepared Traders, Strong Holders

These are longer-term investors with much more experience in most aspects of trading than their amateur colleagues. They have strong portfolios and substantial asset columns, and are active in writing options and selling them to weak holders. They read between the lines of press comments and make up their own minds based on the evidence as they see it. They have long term trading strategies that have worked well for some years, and are interested in results acquired over time. This category incorporates the institutional investors, vast entities skilfully manipulated by the market makers, which give the impression to the outside world that they *are* the market movers. The managers of these institutions deal with huge quantities of money on a daily basis.

The well-prepared trader is the one that has done his homework before entering the market. (He may well have read this book!) He is not led astray by panic or excitement resulting from news in the financial press. He has a tried and tested strategy to which he is faithful because he knows it to deliver results. He is among the minority of traders; that which achieves consistent success.

The Stockbroker

The stockbroker is the person who executes the purchases or sales for the traders. He makes money charging a fee whenever his clients buy or sell. Some brokers provide what is known as a 'full service', giving financial advice as well as executing the trades.

Others provide what is called a 'discount service',

executing trades without offering advice. Clearly, the independent trader who does his own research and makes his own decisions only needs the services of the latter.

The Bulls and Bears

These are not pantomime characters, but traders with different types of outlooks! A 'bear' is a person that believes a stock or commodity market is going to fall and generally has a negative outlook. Bear traders sell stocks, hoping to buy them back when the market falls.

A 'bull' is a person who buys stocks, and plans to sell them at a higher price in the belief that the market will rise. Markets can be described as 'bullish' or 'bearish' depending on whose tendencies are being favoured.

The 'Greek chorus'

In ancient Greek theatre, actors were accompanied by a chorus, which hovered in the background making remarks about what the principal actors were doing, the likely outcome of their actions, and so on. Of course, the audience could see and hear both actors and chorus, but the performers - or, more properly, the characters in the play, paid no attention to the chorus whatsoever, as if they couldn't hear a word of what they were saying.

Just about every trader has his own 'Greek chorus', his family, friends and well-meaning observers of the stockmarket, all of whom monitor the trader's performance, uttering remarks about what is being done and the likely outcome of it.

Trading for a bright future

Many traders make the mistake of listening, and acting according to the advice and often gloomy predictions - making the 'Greek chorus' an important, if generally unrecognised, player in the market. Professional traders, just like the professional Greek actors from long ago, remain calm and oblivious.

Where is Everybody?

A colleague recalled that he could remember all the 'striped jackets' in the cafes and local bars back in the days when buying and selling was always conducted on the trading floor and remarked that these 'trader's bars' today remind him of a ghost town. Computers have taken over the matching of the bids and asks, and there is no longer any real need for the pit traders.

With some notable exceptions, such as Wall Street, most markets, and marketing, occur solely in an electronic environment, so the majority of traders can work from their own office or home, using the services of an on or offline broker to effectuate sales and purchases.

Most of today's traders do not need to put on suits and ties to go to work. They can set up an office for trading in their own home. All of the important markets can simultaneously broadcast information to computer terminals all around the world and online brokering also seems likely to become increasingly important.

Trading for a bright future

•

Although modern trading is almost always an intensely solitary process, it is important to bear in mind that you are one of a vast community of actors in the market. The market has no personality of its own. Whatever character it may be said to have is that of those who work within it - reflecting issues such as cultural differences, etc.

CHAPTER FIVE

What is Being Bought and Sold?

We have already discussed the basic differences between the cash and futures markets. Now, let's take a deeper look at exactly what the traders are buying and selling. Financial terms are so familiar to us on a superficial level, from listening to the news and browsing through papers, that it can be easy to overlook the real meanings of the words that are bandied about.

Bonds are issued by various kinds of institutions, including governments, with the aim of raising capital. Generally, the sale of a bond implies a formal commitment to repay the sum invested, as well as interest, at a certain date in the future.

Contracts are the units of trade in buying and selling futures.

Futures are contracts that require delivery of bonds, commodities, etc. at a specific price, and on a specific date. They are tradable instruments with fluctuating prices, the instruments being contracts that are either settled in cash or delivered as physical bonds or commodities at a specific date in the future. Other instruments such as indices are settled on a specific date relative to the underlying cash value.

Options represent the right to buy or sell a traded particular amount of a stock, property or other commodity. The right to buy is known as a **call option**, and the right to sell a **put option**. An American style traded option represents the right to buy or sell a particular quantity of a stock set or commodity for possible implementation at a specific date or at expiry.

Securities are officially recognised documents - investment instruments - issued by corporations or other organisations as proof of debt or right to equities or other instruments.

A **share** is a legal document indicating that the owner is in possession of one unit of ownership of a company.

A **stock** is a legal document which indicates partial ownership of a company.

How are Purchases and Sales Made?

As you know, a typical trader now works from home or from his personal office, where he observes market behaviour on his computer screen, and makes decisions as to what he is going to buy and sell. The majority of traders still use the services of a stockbroker to actually perform the mechanics of buying and selling, which is done for a fee or percentage. Most stockbrokers also work from computer terminals, and a relatively new option is to use an online brokerage. Before you start trading, you will have chosen a broker and deposited money with him. When you decide what you intend to buy and sell, you instruct him what to do.

Understanding Charts

The proper use of charts is essential to effective technical trading, and to the Bright Futures Strategy which is dealt with in detail later in this book.

Traders can observe the market - whichever one they choose - and make educated decisions about what they are going to do, by using charts. These may look confusing at first, but they are, simply, visual representations of market activity - price fluctuations, purchases and sales. The most revealing tale they tell is of changes in the belief structures of the vast numbers of traders who make up the market. The peaks and troughs represent, not only changes in price, but also the fears and hopes of actors in the market. They illustrate the births, lives and deaths of belief structures.

Chart Anatomy

Charts are composed of a series of lines representing a given period of time, generally drawn in one of the two styles illustrated above; the 'line bar chart' or the 'candle bar chart'. The two styles have identical functions - the difference is essentially aesthetic. Many types of trading software allow the trader to choose which of the two he prefers to use. Charts are more easily drawn using the line bar, and I personally find line bar charts easier to read.

Trading for a bright future

Line Chart and Candle Chart

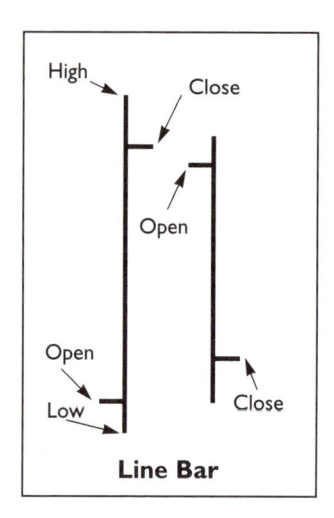

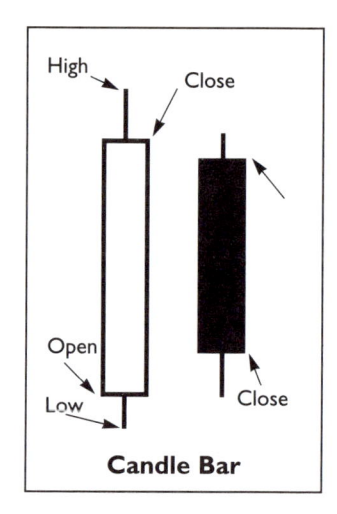

Line Bar

Candle Bar

The horizontal 'branches' that you see on the line bar indicate open and close prices, with the open prices marked on the left and the close prices on the right. The top of the line indicates the highest price reached in the market in the period illustrated, and the bottom of the line indicates the lowest.

Candle bar charts are drawn with white or black bars, illustrating the same information as the line bar charts. The black bars are so coloured to indicate that the close price finished lower than the open.

For me, the more graphic illustration of the candle charts tends to foster an emotional rather than intellectual response to the information about the market, with the risk of affecting my trading performance. You may not have the same reaction, but you should chose which style you prefer, and stick to it.

Next, let's take a look at what the whole chart looks like.

Trading for a bright future

The Ordinary Bar Chart

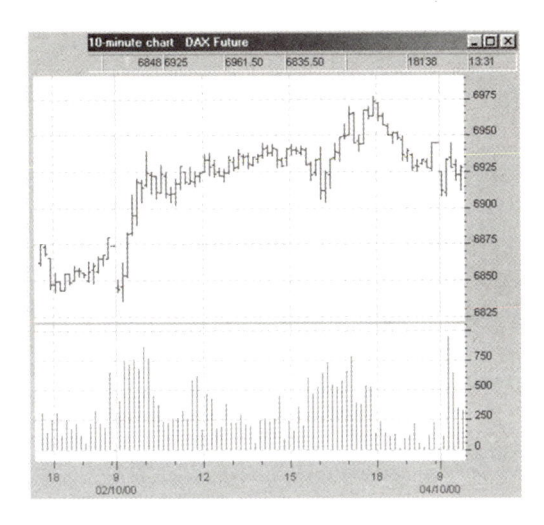

The line bar chart shown above, taken from the DAX market, is drawn using a 10-minute time frame, which means that each bar represents a ten minute time period. Charts can, however, be drawn using practically any period of time.

The vertical bars at the bottom of the window represent the volume of traded business within each ten-minute period. The term 'volume' refers to the amount of market activity taking place at a given moment. The application of this knowledge is discussed in some detail later in this book.

Candle Bar Chart

The candle bar chart, above, represents the same information as the previous illustration. As you can see, the chart looks very different. Don't let aesthetic differences colour your reaction to the information that is displayed.

Trading for a bright future

Tick Charts

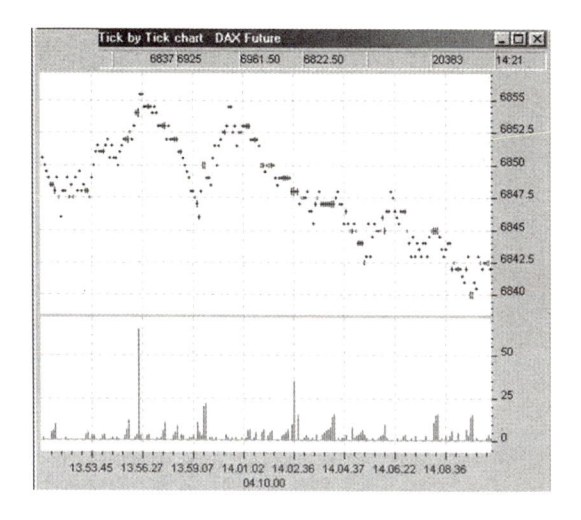

Your first glance at a tick chart may prove confusing, but I know of no type of visualisation of the market that illustrates the action of changing belief patterns in the market more clearly. Each 'tick' or mark which appears on the screen represents a purchase or sale. Using a satellite data feed, traders receive the information in real time, and can watch the peaks and troughs as they are created. Intelligent interpretations of tick charts look beyond price to the belief structures that are contained in the image.

Reading the chart from left to right, the peaks and troughs represent market activity - buying and selling - as the price moves down. This downward movement was quickly reversed as it retraced back to the area where the activity occurred. Subsequently, the reality of the situation is to be seen in a gradually falling price.

The value of the tick chart is that it shows us, not just the point at which market prices changed, but, more importantly, *when and how a new belief about the future price was born.* Never forget that in terms of trading, the perceived value of stock or futures traded outweighs its actual value, and the driving force behind market trends is usually generated by changes in the beliefs of the mass of traders rather than changes in absolute worth.

The important thing to understand from this illustration is the point at which a new belief regarding a future price came into being.

Careful use of a tick chart shows much more than fluctuations in price - you can delve into the collective subconscious of the mass of traders and deduct from their behaviour what it is they believe about the market.

Trading for a bright future

Understanding and Using Volume in Making Trading Decisions

Many traders completely misunderstand or underestimate the potential of volume as a tool in developing a trading strategy, probably because of the variety of ways that it is quoted or interpreted by trading software.

Tick volume, illustrated in the diagram above by the red vertical lines, is simply a count of the price changes over a given period of time.

If you set your software to read tick volume in - for instance - a ten minute bar, then all the computer is doing is adding up all the times that the price changes in that period and building a bar as a histogram within the ten minute time frame.

Quoted volume, on the other hand, is the quoted amount of business that has taken place in a particular period. This volume is perhaps most interesting when it is delivered automatically as the trades take place. This is one of the main advantages in trading a fully electronic market - the information one receives is as clear and uncluttered as it is possible to find.

The application of volume and how it relates to my strategy will be dealt with in the analysis of the strategy itself.

•

Even a relatively brief look at the market demonstrates how complex trading is, and how easily one might get lost in the maze of traders, market makers and the various derivatives including options, futures, and so on. It is important to be prepared, not only with regard to the

47

behaviour of the markets, but also in relation to your own personality and circumstances, and these are the issues that I will discuss next.

CHAPTER SIX

Becoming a Trader - Important Considerations

Now that we have established a clear picture of what the markets are and their workings, it is time to get to the matter at hand; that of turning you into a consistently successful operator within the market. Innumerable would-be traders take the plunge and enter without being properly prepared, either psychologically or in terms of practical information about how the market works. Don't let yourself be one of them! Careful planning and self-awareness are the keys to trading achievement.

To maximise your chances of success, you will need all the right tools. Whether or not you fully realise it, you probably already have the most important of them, as well as the ability to acquire whatever it is you are still lacking. Your most vital task will be to identify your strengths and learn how to use them in the exciting environment of the market, while recognising potential weaknesses and taking measures to counteract them - there is no flaw so great that it cannot be overcome. Mine is to use my own experiences and training to help you to become a successful trader.

When I first began trading, I lost heavily. In fact, at an early stage in my career, I entered the market no less than 32 times *in succession* with losing positions. The odds are so much against this sequence, that it would be hard to

Trading for a bright future

achieve such a 'run of bad luck' on purpose! At that time, I was unable to explain my recurring failure, but now I know that I had become entangled in the wrong loop, or behavioural sequence, and thrown myself onto a self-destructive trading path. With hindsight I can see that, ultimately, my weakness was my strength. The thirty-two failures I initially endured set a course for my turning point and my rebirth as a professional - and successful - trader. Having been a weak holder, I became a strong holder.

The knowledge that I have acquired since then has put me in a position to help you by-pass that frustrating stage. Experience has taught me how to avoid pitfalls, and I can teach you how to maximise your trading potential, giving you at an instant advantage over the novice traders who enter the market unprepared for the surprises that lie ahead.

I hope that you will enter trading with a spirit of optimism, but I don't intend to lead you to believe that trading is easy money in any way. If you decide to take this path, you should be prepared for hard work, frustration and the temptation to give up. Every new challenge is difficult at first, but try to remember that testing times are the crucible that will forge you into a mature, successful trader.

Don't start trading in a real market until you have got a plan of action up and running. Becoming a trader is a big decision to make, and it requires major organisation both *before and during* trading. There is a traditional poem that goes like this;

For want of a nail, the shoe was lost,
For want of the shoe, the horse was lost,
For want of the horse, the rider was lost,

Trading for a bright future

> *For want of the rider, the battle was lost,*
> *For want of the battle, the kingdom was lost,*
> *And all for the want of a horseshoe nail!*

This little piece of folk wisdom is very useful. In planning, whether for doing battle or for trading, *no detail is so small that it can be overlooked,* and even that which seems irrelevant deserves your undivided attention.

Anybody starting out in a conventional business would have a plan - an idea of costs, overheads and profit potential. Most planners would visit their bank manager. Traders should be equally cautious before starting out, but many - if not most - of them are not. One of the reasons for their carelessness comes from the trading environment, which, unlike most businesses, does not demand that you establish a plan.

What does one do before starting a traditional business? Just to mention a few of the vital tasks, any entrepreneur has to make a business plan, arrange bank accounts and financing, make a cash flow forecast and organise accountancy procedures, transport, communications, premises, stock and staff.

When starting out, the typical trader will usually source market data, buy a computer and the necessary software, deposit money with his broker (who needs it to execute trades for him), observe the markets and start trading. As simple as that. Most of the considerations thought to be crucial when starting a traditional business are not included in the typical plans of the budding trader. The financial elements are not present, and an overall plan is completely absent.

Just why doesn't the new trader create a plan? One reason is the somewhat artificial trading environment, which arises from the fact that there are no outside influences. Trading is a very solitary pursuit in this computerised era. You will need to force yourself to ask questions, such as: What if? How many? Expenses? Control? Organisation?

In a more orthodox business environment one is *always* in a position to influence the outcome of any given situation. There is no business component that the individual is unable to influence. One's personal influence creates the manner in which the business is run and ultimately determines its success or failure. *Trading is very different.*

The average trader is unable to influence the outcome of any aspect of trading, and this can cause all sorts of difficulties. Trading is a process undergone alone, and the individual's natural need to control events is turned inward, causing a critical self-examination of psychological characteristics, and creating a forced awareness that can set him up for failure. In this fraught environment, decisions are of utmost importance. Failure to carry out a successful trade throws doubt on the decision-making capabilities of the individual, and the next time that a decision has to be made, the trader is affected by the memory of earlier failures. Decision making capabilities within the trading environment may be systematically destroyed by such personal conflicts.

So what exactly should I do?

If we accept the fact that the trading environment is very different to that of an "ordinary" work environment, we must realise that the skills necessary for success are also distinct. Hence, when you draw up your plans, they must

Trading for a bright future

be tailored specifically towards trading. A well-executed, professional plan is essential, and no factor is so unimportant that it should not receive your full attention. Let's go through the procedure step by step.

First, buy an A4 loose-leaf ring binder, and title it 'My Trading Manual'. Buy a package of separator pages and write 'Basic Concepts', 'Trading Ideas', 'Strategy components/tools', 'Modifications to Strategies', and 'References' on them - you will need these to keep the content in order as your manual expands.

The specific content of your manual is not something that I can dictate to you, as every record is different, and personal to the trader who is keeping it. Generally however, your plan should address the following issues, which you will have to consider both systematically and critically.

- What are your trading aims and ambitions?
- What markets do you intend to trade?
  (futures, options, shares, FOREX, DAX, etc.)
- How much time are you going to devote to your trading?
- Where are you going to trade from?
- What time frames (intra-day, daily, weekly and/or monthly) are you going to trade?
- How much are you prepared to risk in achieving your goals?

Consider each of the questions carefully and calmly before deciding what your answer is. Query your answer. Don't rush these decisions. They are important and should not be

Trading for a bright future

taken lightly. Write down your answer, put it aside and look at it again later. Is there anything you've left out? Keep working at the answer until you are fully satisfied with it. There isn't just one right answer to these questions. Each plan should be tailor-made for the trader in question.

Now, let's address the components that your trading strategy must contain. While everyone is different, there are some key features that are essential.

- Most successful trading systems are *trend-based*[8], if you are going to make profits, you need to follow the overall trend of the market rather than focus on issues such as price. The plan should be simple - a complex one would require a huge amount of work to maintain it, and you will have enough to contend with already. Don't design a strategy that places an extra burden on yourself.

- Your strategy should be *durable* and *flexible*. Market conditions change, and your strategy must be able to adapt to new circumstances. A typical change would be a period of market activity that does not produce a good trend. Your strategy should be able to indicate when the market is unsuitable for you to trade. Any trading strategy should be repeatable - don't base yours on coincidence. Test it on

---

[8] The issue of understanding trends is fully explained in a later chapter. The word 'most' is used here advisedly - there are some successful trading strategies that are *not* trend-based, although these are less common.

Trading for a bright future

paper in diverse market conditions before venturing into the real market.

- Be *objective* in your interpretation of signals. If you are looking for three certain actions to take place in a given order, then *that* is your strategy. If you find yourself questioning the validity of any given element, you have introduced subjectivity and set a bad precedent.
  If you introduce a new element, your *complete* strategy must be tested and validated again.

- Your strategy should give *no relevance to price*. Price should merely reflect the fact that a transaction between you and the person from whom you bought or to whom you have sold has taken place. Buying or selling on the basis of price alone, is 'price trading' not 'strategy trading'. Price is an *emotive and destructive element*, and is never of itself a reason to enter or exit a market.

- Consider how you are going to monitor your trading. Once you enter a trade, you are in the market until your strategy determines the time to exit. This may be, for instance, a simple stop loss order, a moving average crossover, sudden high volume, or whatever your strategy contains.
  You may wonder why there is a need to monitor your trade when the strategy should determine all your actions. Imagine the following scenario: You are in the market; your trade is now some forty points in the money and your original stop

loss order is way below the market. This will need to be moved up to the last reaction. This is the process of monitoring your trade.

- It is important to note that the moving of your stop must fall within your tested strategy. For example, if you move a stop up to the last reaction, this action should be tested within your overall strategy. The issue of designing a suitable strategy is discussed in more detail later in the text.

- Keep a trading log. It will become your most valuable asset. While amateur traders record prices, profitable professionals keep journals and records, not only of each trade but also of all the steps they actioned throughout. From this journal, you will be able to hone and improve your strategy. It does require discipline, and you will have to be prepared to accept the possibility that it will highlight flaws in your strategy that you may be unwilling to acknowledge.

Types of Trades

An **intra-day trade** is one that results from trading activity lasting for part of a day, or for a day, according to the amount of profit sought. A **short-term trade** involves staying in the market for a period of time in order to reap the profits of a larger price move. A **medium** or **long-term trade** is when the trader holds on to his stock for a considerable length of time and through large price changes. Some traders prefer to work just one type of trade, while others are interested in the full range. While the basic mechanisms for making a trade - observing the market, making a decision, and telling your broker to perform an action - remain the same, the details are very different. For intra-day trading, one observes market actions within a single day, together with selective use of longer time frames, including day or week charts. Trading activity, as such, is confined within the limits of the day. Longer term tactics involve observing market trends over greater periods of time.

Trading Tools

Great care must be taken when selecting tools, which include the broker, the datafeed and its associated analysis tools. Quality varies considerably in each of these categories, and companies come and go. While the advice given here will be helpful, you should not neglect to research everything thoroughly by yourself.

To begin trading you will need a charting software package that provides you with a range of technical indicators - short-term trends used to predict future movements of securities or commodities - which you will be able to customise in the developing of a strategy designed around your circumstances. This will enable you to make intelligent, informed decisions. A wide range of charting packages are available, many of which may be downloaded from the Internet. The use of software or other systems to predict market trends is known as 'technical analysis' and involves the use of charts. The trader needs to chart the price of a stock or index within a period of

Trading for a bright future

time and use trend lines (lines drawn between visual depictions of market peaks and troughs, illustrating overall movements), and analysis to become able to predict what is likely to happen in the future.

The type of chart most commonly used by traders is the **bar chart**, which gives the high, low, opening and closing prices of the stock over a particular period of time, and illustrates its trading range.

Apart from a charting package, there are many other types of software for you to choose from, including market data providers, which bring information such as quotes and market information to your desktop. Individual markets generally offer links to software, often with backup staff available to provide technical assistance.

Choosing the right software can be a daunting business, simply because of the sheer number of options available. Fortunately, many offer a thirty-day trial period with the programme before you have to pay, giving you some time to test it before you make a decision. Software is generally designed to work with one of the well-known computer systems, such as Windows from Microsoft, and it is important that your computer is kept up to date so as to be able to deal with innovations as they emerge.

Your initial outlay, in terms of buying a computer, the relevant software, etc., can be quite large, but remember that many programs offer updates on the internet, either for free or for very reasonable prices. By and large, there is no need for any expert help in downloading software from the internet or installing it on your computer, if you feel you can't manage it yourself,

Trading for a bright future

you may be sure one of the children will have it sorted out in moments!

Market information is available via the Internet, but to ensure the most accurate representation and delivery of this information, traders really need a satellite datafeed. Generally, dealing through the Internet is fast and efficient, and data sent via the Internet is very popular at the time of writing. It offers portability and in some cases, integration with your dealing system.

However, data sent this way is subject to the problems associated with the medium, and even the best connections in the United States suffer the occasional 'brownout', or internet data traffic jam. At these times, you should switch back to using your desk broker or stop trading for that period. It is very wise to have at least two ISP backups ready to go at any time, and it is often worth paying to get a better internet service when dealing - one that may not be so busy with traffic.

The 'brownouts' - periods when there are delays in the transmission of data - are far less likely to occur in the case of satellite data. Many data feeds are now building the ability to chart the market directly into their software. This offers some significant benefits, such as the instant update of the data to the chart. Some software packages still require a linking database that connects the data feed with the trading charting software.

The most important feature of the datafeed is that it sends all the data in real time. This might sound like stating the obvious but, in fact, there are more than a few available that either miss out some data - in some cases a considerable amount - or send it delayed, or both.

Trading for a bright future

One decisive factor in choosing a datafeed system is cost. Not everyone can afford the luxury of being in a fixed location and in a reception area, and traders in this situation are probably well advised to look into an Internet service. The following are some of the popular datafeeds currently available:

QuoteSpeed
www.thedatafeedshop.com

This datafeed offers timely, comprehensive updates on European and US markets, with excellent satellite and internet coverage. The charting facility is excellent and while the product quality may not be up to, for example, that of CQG (discussed below), the standard is very good, as is the level of support from the agent and the company.

CQG (Commodity Quote Graphics)
www.cqg.com

This datafeed carries a range of US and global futures markets, but carries little comprehensive stock data. Charting, support and timeliness are generally excellent. However the service costs rather more than QuoteSpeed, which is almost as good.

e Signal
www.esignal.com

Unlike the Signal satellite service, which cannot currently be recommended because of problems with speed, e Signal offers an excellent service at a reasonable price. Similar in price to QuoteSpeed and Market Eye, its market coverage is more US oriented, as it covers for example, NASDAQ Level II. Its current coverage of European markets is not very comprehensive.

Choosing a Broker

Your broker may be electronic or manual. Ideally however, you will be offered either option or a combination of the two. A purely electronic broker usually offers an Internet based service, via the broker's computer directly into the exchange dealing computer. This is known as 'electronic trading'. Some brokers offer electronic only dealing, which means you can't call the broker if something goes wrong.

Large brokers such as Mann, Lind Waldock, Reffco, GNI and Linnco offer *either* the old fashioned desk broking, *or* electronic broking with desk backup (useful when you are out or something goes wrong). Their clients are offered the best of both worlds. The following are some of the points that you should bear in mind when choosing a broker.

- Make sure your broker is polite at all times, and does not comment on your trades, especially if he is an 'execution only' broker. Remarks such as "really", "well done," and so on, are unnecessary, and can be distracting. If your broker does this kind of thing, either ask him not to, or consider closing the account. His job is to be totally professional and impersonal at all times.

Trading for a bright future

- Be wary of small brokers. If you use the services of one, one day you may find that the business has gone bankrupt - something that happens much more frequently than many suspect. Even with regulators and insurance, recovering trading capital - or a portion of it - can take months, or in some cases years.

- Make sure that you trade with a reputable, efficient company, especially if you are dealing with large sums. For example, it is unlikely that a broker owned by a national bank will default. Fimat Futures is an example of such a type of broker. Owned by a successful French bank, Societe General (SocGen), this is one of the best, and is all but backed by the national government. Similarly, in the unusual event of a large bank crashing, it is unlikely that the national government would not bail it out.

- Medium sized brokers do not usually go bankrupt, but it has been known to happen. However, such companies often offer traders the best deals. When you are looking into using the services of a medium sized broker, you should be wary of companies that ask for a monthly minimum trade size, as you may want to go away for a while.

- A modern broker should be able to email as well as 'snail mail' your contract notes to you.

Trading for a bright future

- If the broker starts to make frequent mistakes, such as posting other peoples' trades to your account, there is something wrong. My advice is to change broker.

- Any dealing room worth your investment should answer the phone on the first or, at most, second ring. Brokers who go home early, give vague answers, and cannot answer questions easily and competently should be viewed with suspicion.

- Make sure that the broker you are dealing with is regulated. In the Middle East, Far East, Germany, Switzerland and many other places, brokers are either lightly regulated or not regulated at all. Should any problem arise, you are at his mercy - and so is your money.

- Never forget that to most brokers you are simply a number, another client. Your wins or losses are of no consequence to him. So far as he is concerned, you simply generate commission and move on. Your relationship is not a personal one. You, for your part, have a perfect right to expect efficiency, fast execution, reliability and polite behaviour.

- Assess your tax situation very carefully. It is worth consulting with at least one tax expert to make sure that you do not end up giving all your hard-earned profits back to a tax authority.

Trading for a bright future

You need to feel confident that you can trust your broker, so don't just opt for the first one that comes along. Investing money and time in a brokerage is not to be taken lightly. Shop around until you feel confident that you have found someone that you can really trust. Even if you think that you have found the professional for you, don't hesitate to interview the candidate in order to find out about his or her qualifications, experience and approach to work. Investigate the true costs of an account with the professional or firm - sometimes low commissions conceal hidden costs elsewhere. You need to have ready access by phone to your brokerage. Will you be provided with assistance when and if you need it? Can the brokerage offer help and advice on subjects such as research and trading tools?

If you are going to use a human broker as your point of contact, make sure that he doesn't have to phone a third party to execute trades in an electronic market. It is important that he can execute trades for you directly and immediately.

In choosing a broker many traders make hasty leaps of faith. The wisdom of conducting at least preliminary research should speak for itself.

Communicating Effectively with your Broker

It is important to know how to communicate with your broker. He will appreciate it if you can keep your requests concise and specific, and it is your money that is on the line so you have certainly got a vested interest in knowing that there is no confusion about what it is you want!

There are a number of types of basic orders. A **market**

order is the most frequently used type. It is carried out at the best possible price available at the time the order is traded. Its greatest use is in ensuring that the customer does not have to invest much effort 'chasing' the market, and trying to get in and out of a position.

The advantage of a market order is that you will get in at the next available price. This is very useful when you need to get in or out quickly as when the market is moving very quickly. The disadvantage is that you will not be able to 'work' the order to extract a better price from the market (as is often possible when the market is moving slowly in a tight range). In such cases a limit order can be employed.

A **limit order** is an order to buy or sell at a pre-arranged price. Limit orders to sell are placed above the market; those to buy are placed below the market, as there is no guarantee that the market will go high or low enough to fill the order. If the market is falling or rising away from you rapidly, either place a limit well inside what you think you will get (to save yourself from being filled at *absolutely* any price, as is the case with a market order) or use a market order to make sure of getting out, because by the time you have another chance to change your limit, the market may have moved well away from your price.

More importantly though, limit orders can be used during volatile conditions to get a fill at a better price when the market is violently oscillating between prices in a close range, so that the broker *must* execute the order if the price trades even one tick above or below your sell or your buy 'at limit' order. Limit orders, if intelligently and realistically placed, can save hundreds of pounds. This is their real power, especially on floor traded markets.

Trading for a bright future

Their use effectively prevents unscrupulous market makers and the like filling your order at a price that suits them, not you!

Let's take a look at an example of the effective use of a limit order. Suppose that the E Mini S&P is quoted with a 1386 bid and a 1387.50 offer (ask) price. In this case, if the trader wants to sell immediately, he can hit the offer at 1386, as someone is definitely willing to buy at this price. What happens when an offer is entered into the system at 1387.00, with the hope of a sale at a higher price? Imagine that the current offer of 1387.50 is the best sell price on the system for someone who wants to be sure of buying. But the moment an offer to sell at 1387 is entered, all the quote screens around the world instantly offer that instrument at 1387 - a better price for a buyer - instead of the previous 1387.50. 1386 will then be the nearest sure place to make a sale. In an electronically matched market the trader effectively acts as a market maker. He can make an inside price, and when someone enters a market order to buy, he will instantly be matched with the next best available price to sell. The initial trader gets traded at 1387 to sell, a full point above 1386. Should there be no other offers in the system, the screen instantly offers 1387.50 again as the best offered price.

In the markets when an offer or bid has been taken up, it is said to have been hit. This process is how markets are made. For example, if someone keeps hitting the offer/ask price, the price moves to the next higher seller. This can lead to price spikes of many points. In one example I observed recently[9], someone spiked the E Mini S&P from 1348 to 1380 in five seconds. He kept buying all the offers,

[9] Just before the close of business on January 4th, 2001.

Trading for a bright future

and soon the next offer was way above the market. It was hit and ten seconds later the market was back at 1355. In less than a minute, the market saw as much activity as it often sees in a while day.

The type of activity I describe is sometimes the result of professionals 'running the stops'. It occurs when a couple of traders artificially run the market up, triggering all the buy stop orders above the market in order to get people long (buying) way above the real market.[10] For example, if there is an electronic system that can see a buy order at 1375, then the market can be artificially taken up by arranging that someone will take out all the offers on the way up, resulting in trading occurring at a much higher price. The market reacts by returning to its real value, leaving the person who traded at the higher price, stopped in with a huge loss. All this is infrequent, but possible - so be careful!

A **stop order** is used for three basic reasons. To minimise a loss on a long or short position (respectively, anticipating a rise or fall in prices), to protect a profit on an existing long or short position, or to initiate a new long or short position. A buy stop order is placed above the market and a sell stop order is placed below the market. Once the stop price is touched, the order will be treated like a market order, and will be filled at the best possible price.

Most traders use stop orders either to limit loss or to lock in a profit. A stop order to enter the market allows you to let the market prove itself by moving towards your (in this instance) buy order.

A **market if touched order**, often referred to as an **MIT**,

---

[10] Such unethical practices were common in the old FTSE dealing pit, when LIFFE was still a floor traded market.

is the opposite of a stop order. A **buy MIT** is placed below the market and a **sell MIT** is placed above the market. This type of order is generally used to enter the market or to begin a trade. Once the limit price is touched or passed, the MIT order becomes a market order and can be carried out at, above or below the specified price. The order is not executed if the market fails to touch the MIT specified price.

An **OCO** or **one cancels the other order** is a combination of two orders. Once one side of the order is filled, the remaining side should be cancelled. By placing two instructions on one order, the trader cuts out the possibility of a double fill.

If you assume that the instrument you are trading is currently at 100 and you would like to buy into this market at 110, you should say "Buy me one *(name of instrument)* on stop at 110." This order is instructing your broker to buy you one contract / share, etc. if the price touches 110.

A **stop limit order** is a way of limiting damage by specifying that the broker should sell or buy your order at a specific price, and not a lower one. The danger lies in the possibility that the market will bypass your stop and you will not be filled at all, but exposed to more loss.

When **slippage** occurs, you are not filled at your specified price. For example, when you have a stop in the market at - for example - 95, and the market trades at 92, and is then followed by a rapid price movement through 95 to 99, the three points difference would be termed slippage. Slippage generally occurs when the market is moving very quickly and the sheer volume of business forces the broker to get you in or out of the market at the best possible price that he can, rarely far from your original order. Stop limit orders avoid the occurrence of slippage, but the market must actually trade at the limit price to ensure that you are filled. Should it gap through the price you specified rather than trade there, your order may not be filled.

The Work Area

Remember 'for the want of a nail'? Don't overlook the important detail of your trading environment. As you know, few traders ever need to set foot on a trading floor, and almost everybody works from their remote computer terminal. This brings to mind the important issue of your office - and it *is* important. Working from home has some major advantages - you can set up an office in your house at very little cost - no extra heating or electricity bills, no transport costs - but a home office is not necessarily for everybody. Parents of young children may find their attention distracted, and end up being unfair to both work and family. There is always the temptation to return to your computer when the work day should really be over, or to leave your work-space when you should be concentrating to attend to some family matter that could really wait until later. For some, a separate work space is necessary to achieve the psychological distance essential to clear minded trading. If working at home is liable to cause stress, you should seriously consider other options. A stressed trader is not a good one, and a stressed family member is equally ineffective. If you do decide to work at home, set clear boundaries in terms of space and time - and stick to them. If you feel that a home office is a potential source for stress and disturbance, renting an office elsewhere is a possibility that might be viable, particularly for those who intend to trade full-time.

Another item that is definitely not too insignificant to mention is the question of physical comfort. An orthopaedic chair is an excellent investment - just try making level headed decisions when your back is aching. Natural light is also much to be desired. Take a break from your computer at least every hour or so to rest your eyes. Be careful to get some physical exercise during your working day - brains as well as bodies become sluggish if the whole system is not given an opportunity to work out. Those involved in any sedentary job should ensure that their working space has plenty of fresh air, that the atmosphere does not become too dry and that they themselves do not become dehydrated - keep plenty of drinking water on hand.

•

Many new traders, having made the momentous decision to enter the market, are so eager to begin that they start trading without having made all the necessary plans. Getting organised may not be glamorous or exciting, but every hour that you invest in careful planning will be repaid in market success.

In locating both broker and a datafeed you need to search for speed and efficiency. Without speed you are at a severe disadvantage in the intraday market. Making trading decisions and taking actions on data that is historical in nature is not a winning approach. Successful trading demands a timely reaction to an unfolding situation. You need a broker that gets you out fast when things start to go wrong and in quickly when opportunity beckons. Similarly, you need a datafeed that *always* reports what is happening *now*. Price is important, but so is quality of service. As standards change constantly, keep ensuring that you are getting the service you deserve in executing your strategy.

Most importantly, in your preparations you should never forget that there is no detail so minor that you can afford to overlook it.

Trading for a bright future

CHAPTER SEVEN

Managing your Personal Circumstances

In a later chapter, I will discuss the technical side of the market in still more detail and examine some strategies that you can use to maximise your profit margin. However, of at least equal importance to such matters are the attitudes and personal characteristics that you take with you into the market.

The issue of personality is a fascinating one, and psychologists and social scientists of all kinds agree on at least one point – it is an infinitely complex subject. We are all the products of our genes, our upbringing and all the things we have experienced throughout our lives.

In trading, it is important to recognise one's innate tendencies - not to be judgmental, not to see if you are the 'wrong sort of person' to go into trading - but to identify potential problems *before* they are manifested in an uncontrolled fashion.

Another important point that is easily overlooked is that nobody is alone in this world - we are all surrounded by family, friends and acquaintances and, being the emotive beings we are, we are influenced by them - by our desires to impress, please or even anger them.

These facts, together with practical issues such as funding and planning, affect in no small measure our abilities in the challenging trading sphere. New traders are willing to devote time to choosing office equipment and software, but all too often they neglect to sit down and think carefully of these other, even more important issues - perhaps because they are afraid of what they might have to admit.

Before we examine the technical aspects of the market, stop and examine your own, personal, potential strengths and weaknesses as a trader. Everybody's circumstances are different, and many types of people can go on to become successful traders, pending careful planning.

Funding

One is often cautioned by the well intended to trade strictly within one's means. This overly pessimistic approach presupposes failure, and while you should certainly take sensible precautions, that can hardly be the right way to embark upon an important new career! Of course, care should be taken so that you won't end up in an awkward financial situation, but be positive.

If you need to make a living from trading, my advice is that you ensure that you have living expenses for at least a year in a safe account. Quite apart from being the sensible thing to do, this will remove a lot of personal pressure that could easily affect your decision making and overall performance as a trader. Lack of sufficient funds can cause traders to hold positions for longer than they should, in the hope that the market will turn and give them back their money. Of course, there is no guarantee that this will happen, and frequently it does not, resulting in an untenable situation.

Trading for a bright future

Case Study

Seán, at thirty-four years old, was a relatively successful assistant manager at a large supermarket in a provincial city. He had developed a keen interest in the markets over several years and felt that he was ready to start trading. They had three small children, and as his wife had stopped working to care for them, Seán's salary had to support the whole family. Feeling that he was letting his youth pass him by without having realised any of his major ambitions, Seán took a big step. He decided to leave his job, and taking up trading full time. A year before, he had inherited ten thousand pounds, and he invested this money in a computer and the necessary software to embark upon his new career. Seán had always studied the newspapers for trading news, and felt confident that he would succeed. Jane was anxious, but supportive.

Seán started trading, and had enjoyed modest success for over three months, earning about 60% of what he had been making in the supermarket. He tried to tell himself to be patient, and that no-one can make a huge amount of money at once, but he was all too aware that there was only enough money in the bank to keep the family for two or three months more. Every time he made a trade, his anxiety levels rose to such an extent that he was unable to think clearly and his results - less than satisfactory to begin with - became more and more erratic.

After three months, Seán felt that he simply could not carry in this manner. He had to admit defeat and sought out conventional work. This situation need never have come about if proper planning and strategy implementation had been carried out.

How Can Other People Influence Your Trading?

Never underestimate the effect of your family and friends on your attitude and overall performance. In ideal circumstances, they can help you win. In less than ideal, they can contribute to professional catastrophe.

Of course, everybody's personal circumstances are different, but take care not to overlook the possible dangers. Sit down and think about it. What does your spouse or partner think of the prospect of your trading? Does he or she dismiss it as gambling? Are you the sort of person to be overly affected by the opinions of others? If the answer to any of these questions is 'yes', the negative environment you are in may seriously affect your performance, and you need to redress this by ensuring that your professional life as a trader is kept completely separate from such concerns. It is important to identify and deal with potential problems *before* they happen. Don't let yourself get dragged down by another person's pessimism. More than one trader has ended up having to choose between continuing to trade and getting divorced, or stopping and staying married, so try to plan things well. Trading can appear to be a drug at times, and for those close to a trader it can become a nightmare.

Case Study

When her children were born, Mary decided to leave her job and become a full-time mother, but now that she was forty-eight, Sam and Yvonne were older and more independent and she had more time on her hands. She started to devote a couple of hours every day to something

Trading for a bright future

that had always been a hobby; studying the market and 'paper trading'. Mary had always had a flair for numbers and forward planning, and after several months of practice she felt confident that she'd hit on a strategy that would work for her in the real market. Her husband did his best to dissuade her from trading. He was inclined to be over-protective, and was afraid that she would be crushed if it didn't work out.

"Besides," he reasoned, "I make a good living as an accountant, so we don't need an extra income."

Despite David's attempts to influence her, Mary did start trading, confident that she would succeed. To her dismay, things did not go nearly as well as expected, and she made more and more ill-judged decisions every day.

Mary is a very determined person, so she sat down to think about what might be going wrong. She and David were a very close couple, and always listened to each other. In this case, she had taken his misgivings about her trading on board. The pressure of having to show him that she could succeed despite his doubts was having a very detrimental effect on her performance, and she had grown to dread the family's evening meal when he would ask her how everything was going. Mary decided it would be better simply to avoid discussing her trading with her husband at all. He accepted this, and agreed never to ask unless she brought up the subject herself.

With the pressure gone, Mary began to enjoy real trading as much as she'd enjoyed paper trading, and pending some adjustments here and there, her strategy worked well. David often admits that the most important stage for Mary was when he allowed her freedom of thought to take her own decisions, regardless of the outcome.

Deal With Other People in a Positive Manner

No-one is ever going to completely share your point of view or way of understanding things, no matter how hard to try to make them. If you feel that you *must* explain and justify yourself, keep it simple. Never attempt to manipulate someone else into providing a support system for you - that is a recipe for disappointment. You will need to decide up to what point you are prepared to discuss your trading, and you should avoid involving another person in your professional decisions.

Don't let your personal trading-related feelings of anger, frustration or elation seep into your private life. To let this happen would be unfair to you as a professional, and to those with whom you share your life. If people ask, restrain yourself to simple statements such as "It was a good day" or "It was a productive day in terms of learning" - they'll soon learn that there are some things you would prefer not to discuss.

Case Study

Matthew, at twenty-five years old, had a consuming passion about becoming a trader and making trading his way of life. He decided that he didn't want to spend the rest of his life in an ordinary office job, and so he enrolled on a course or two and even completed a set of city examinations that left him far more technically qualified than many traders.

He prudently followed the markets for several months before handing in his resignation at the auctioneers' firm where he worked. All of his friends were curious, and when Matthew met up with them in the evenings to have a beer and play darts, they would all ask him how it was going, what he thought would happen to such and such a stock, whether he could recommend an investment to them, and so on.

At first Matthew was very flattered that others were asking for his opinion, but eventually he realised that the process of finding answers was dissipating his own energy and judgement. He took a very decisive step in ceasing to vocalise his impression of the market. He reasoned that when everybody else went out in the evening, they left their work behind them, and that he should do the same. He kept his answers curt, and changed the subject to talk about hobbies, football, and other things of general interest.

It had never occurred to him that trading might affect his relationship with his friends. Some were offended at first, but eventually they learned that their questioning brought forth less and less from Matthew. He in turn gained strength and more commitment to what he was doing and to his overall goals.

Have a Well-Defined Strategy

If you are lacking a well-defined strategy, you will be left wandering aimlessly without an idea of where you should go or how you should get there. This can only result in an enormous loss of time - and money. You must develop a strategy that you trust completely, so that you can act according to it without doubts or hesitations. This book will help you to do just that.

Trading for a bright future

Case Study

Ian had been working in the market for more than a year when he realised that he was simply going to have to stop. Repeated losses were affecting not only his trading but also his relationship with his wife, daughters, and friends. When he began, he had been careful to put aside enough money to fall back on and he had felt confident that he would be able to succeed.

At first, trading went well and he made several handsome profits. After three months, however, he was beginning to make more losses than gains, and had to cut into the security money that he had saved. As the pressure increased, Ian started to panic, to make hasty decisions and to take any profits he had succeeded in making out of the market straight away. He became stressed and tired, and as he reached the end of his first year of trading, was cursing himself and the market to anyone that would listen.

The reason why Ian failed lay in his lack of a strategy. His chaotic approach left him unable to deal rationally with occasional losses and vulnerable to panic attacks and decisions based on emotion rather than reason. If he had given time to developing a strategy, there is every reason to suppose that he would have been successful at his first attempts to trade the market.

When Ian started to look at the market again after having spent some time away from it, he realised that he did have the basis of a strategy. Other elements were letting him down. Ian is now well on his way to polishing his strategy and honing the skills that will turn him into a successful trader.

Trading for a bright future

Be Your Own Trader!

The press is an important influencing factor in the professional life of a trader. Let's assume that you have decided not to let newspapers affect your decisions, and that you will be influenced purely on the evidence that you have accrued. But as you sip your coffee and browse through your daily paper, you notice that a certain group will be meeting today to announce some new finance measures. Later, you notice a market action you don't fully understand, and search for an explanation. Whether you wish it or not, you recall the story you read, and the *very act of remembering* causes you to be influenced. You may find it difficult to trade, and your interpretation of the evidence gathered will have been affected. Avoid letting this happen, and similarly avoid being led astray by phone calls 'just to let you know about something that is going on'.

Another dangerous area you should be aware of is that of expressing your opinion about market movements. Let me present you with another scenario. Someone calls and asks for your professional opinion. This appeals to your sense of pride and you offer an explanation for certain market activities. The act of doing so engraves an opinion in stone in your mind. You are no longer flexible, and even if the evidence before you suggests that you were incorrect, it will be difficult to change.

No-one is more easily won over to someone's opinion than oneself. Voicing your opinion can cause you to prevent to take action based on the real evidence as it reveals itself. My advice is that whenever anyone asks you what you think the market is going to do, is simply to state the truth; 'whatever it likes at any given moment'.

Case Study

Latifah had amazed everyone in managing to turn a profit in her first three months of trading. Others who sometimes dabbled in the markets, as well as a few friends and relatives impressed by her success, thought that they might benefit from her 'expert' advice. Almost every day someone rang her to see what she thought about this or that trading possibility and to find out what way she thought the market was going to turn.

Latifah, when she was being honest, had to admit that she enjoyed the attention, and when several pieces of advice turned out to be helpful, it felt good. But in the process, she forgot to pay attention to her strategy. It wasn't long before she had given out some advice that did neither her nor her friend any favours, and she realised that making claims for the market's behaviour is a risky business. Fortunately, this realisation didn't come too late to save her from a total trading disaster, and she managed to get back on track - and never let herself be tempted to voice her opinions out loud again. She has turned into one of the most secretive and non-opinionated traders that I know. She is one who is destined for huge success.

Taking Early Profits and Accepting Losses as Part of the Trading Process

In a fair world, the crime of taking early profits would be prohibited by law! Nonetheless, there are many reasons why people make this fatal mistake. Some are unwilling to accept a loss, others have under-capitalised. More have allowed themselves to fall under the unhelpful influence of someone else, or have failed in developing a strategy. Rather than putting yourself in a situation that will cause you to be tempted, ensure that you are prepared to avoid making this mistake.

The trader who is unwilling to accept a loss puts himself at a disadvantage. Situations will arise in which you simply need to accept that loss is inevitable. For some people this is difficult, especially in a situation where a strong opinion about what is likely to happen has already been voiced. Never interpret a loss as an attack against you. The market is impersonal and as a trader, you should be too.

Case Study

Amajit had always been deeply competitive. Even as a child, he had never been able to take 'no' for an answer, and throughout school he reacted badly to failure, always trying to be the first in the class. Not winning a race, or excelling in an exam always made him feel that he had failed on a personal level. In some ways, Amajit's attitude was one of his strengths, but when he decided to start trading, he did not assess the possible dangers it represented.

He was advised to accept that occasional losses are part of trading, but dismissed this advice as being irrelevant to him - and when he experienced them was enraged by what he felt were his own shortcomings. In an ill-judged attempt to prevent losses, He started to withdraw early profits in an attempt to prevent himself from being wrong, this act of taking early profits and closing winning trades had driven him into a corner, and he was forced to leave trading before returning with a much changed personal attitude towards himself and his earlier 'perceived' wrong trades.

Understanding How Markets Work

The trader that does not have a comprehensive understanding of how markets work is at a serious disadvantage, and you owe it to yourself not to enter trading without having addressed this issue. For example, trading futures without properly understanding the nature of contract expiry could cause any number of problems. Traders must fully understand the market in general, and especially the particular aspect of the market with which they deal, if they wish to operate successfully. Be prepared.

Case Study

Susan's ten years of work as a personal assistant in an editing company didn't seem like a particularly good start to profitable trading, but during the eighteen months prior to her resignation she had spent most of her free time studying the market until she felt confident enough to start trading. After several months of research, Susan decided that trading currencies was the option that appealed most, and she explored this area until she was a real expert on the subject. Her organised approach worked well and she now enjoys a level of independence that she could never have achieved through secretarial work - as well as a much higher income. Her only regret is that she didn't start trading years ago, when dissatisfaction at being at someone's beck and call first set in.

She can now look back and realise that her strength lies in her firm understanding of her chosen market and an ongoing commitment to personal development.

Trading for a bright future

Trust yourself and manage fear of what the market may or may not hold

Failure to trust oneself in the market is invariably the result of not understanding the process of trading. Imagine that you start working, with your strategy in place, when suddenly the trade reacts in a manner inconsistent with what you expected. As the trade nears your stop you find that your anxiety levels are soaring. Why? You are committed to your tried and tested strategy. You *know* it succeeds more often than it fails. Let's examine a number of the factors that cause confidence failure.

Imagine that you enter the market using the strategy that you have developed. You are confident that the trade is good, when suddenly it reacts in a manner that you had not anticipated. As the trade approaches your stop, you become increasingly anxious. Why? You have tried and tested your strategy and have every reason to be confident in it. Are you under-funded? To be so puts you in a highly stressful situation, in which fear of failure overcomes your trust in your strategy. Are you using a strategy which you feel, either consciously or subconsciously, to be untested? Have you traded outside your strategy? This last possibility generally arises from the trader's sense of frustration when the market does not permit the use of his or her own strategy. In such a circumstance, the trader tends to look around for something that appears consistent with the tested strategy before trading. I refer to this as 'stepping outside the strategy'. It is a very destructive position to take, and may cause damage that will take many weeks to repair.

Fear also springs from incomplete understanding.

Case Study

Paul had always had a problem with self-confidence. Sadly, he didn't address this potential issue properly before starting trading. This situation led to immense stress. Whenever he made a profit, he would wonder if he'd ever be able to do it again, and whenever he lost, he felt, glumly, that it was inevitable. Hardly surprising then, that Paul's failure to understand the repercussions of his personality led to a swift disappearance of the capital set aside for what he had hoped would be a great new venture. If he had been more honest with himself, he would have recognised the probability of his failure to trust himself affecting his trading, and could have taken steps to counteract it.

Unfortunately, Paul's failure in trading only served to strengthen his negative self-image, imperfect understanding of his character and his fear in the trading environment. Both his trading failure and the crisis of confidence it brought about could have been avoided with forward planning.

Through diligent personal exploration and working towards a deeper understanding of himself and his psychological make-up Paul is making great strides in becoming the type of trader that he wants to - and *can* - become.

How to Avoid Anxiety about your Trading Performance
Be consistent

If you are already trading and you are in a *losing loop*, discard it and create a new one. If you are a new trader, make sure you construct a *winning loop* from the outset, and stay in it!

Once you have developed and tested a profitable trading strategy, you should act upon it. This advice might sound too obvious even to mention, but there are lots of factors that can cause inconsistent behaviour, such as personal conflict regarding the strategy on a conscious or subconscious level. This can be the result of poor testing of the strategy or of disavowal of certain parts of it, of a lack of trading capital, or of a tendency to delay trading, because the trade just out of reach seems more attractive - something that I like to refer to as 'cherry picking'. The bottom line, however, is that there are as many reasons for inconsistency as there are traders. If you start to notice inconsistency slipping in to your work, stop, calm down and ask yourself why. Once you have identified the cause, you will be able to take the appropriate actions.

Case Study

Lee felt that he was ready to trade - he had tested his strategy thoroughly, placed money in the bank and with his broker and bought all the necessary equipment and software. He was sure that nothing had been overlooked. But when he started trading, he ran into trouble. He was always sure that a better option was just around the corner, and often failed to take the actions that his strategy indicated. Fortunately, his reaction to his patchy results was to take a calm look at what was going on. Once he identified the reason for his inconsistent behaviour, he was able to take the appropriate steps to combat it, and is now trading successfully on a full-time basis.

Trading for a bright future

His turning point came when he realised that the problem was not with his planning or strategy but within himself. A short period of complete personal analysis was all that was needed to turn the corner.

•

Are you feeling overwhelmed? Nothing is ever easy at first, but as we continue, concepts and terms will become more familiar to you, and you will begin to learn how to apply this new information to your trading and your life. Before you continue to read, I suggest that you sit down with pen and paper and make a list of your potential strengths and shortcomings. Identifying these will be an important step forward, because the psychological make-up of the individual trader is *at least* as important as his level of understanding of the markets. Potential weaknesses are not, of themselves, a reason not to trade - careful planning can turn weaknesses into strengths. Don't be ashamed or embarrassed of your emotional side - recognise it as a fundamental part of what you are and embrace its weaknesses as well as its strengths. You might even consider asking someone who knows you very well what they think might be your potential weaknesses in trading. One is not always entirely honest with oneself!

CHAPTER EIGHT

Getting down to Business

By now, you have achieved a number of important goals. You understand how the market works and how the important people in it function. You have carefully assessed yourself and your personal circumstances, and you know what you will need to do in order to become a successful trader. You have recognised your potential strengths and weaknesses and you are ready to acquire a more detailed knowledge of market dynamics, and to learn how to view market activity from a position above the crowd.

Trading for a bright future

Supply and Demand in the Cash Market

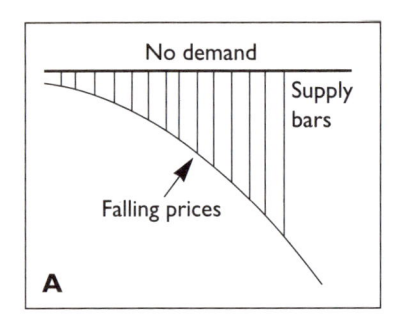

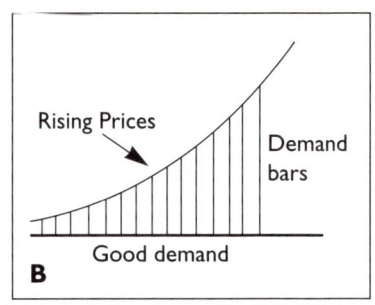

A: No demand / Supply bars / Falling prices

B: Rising Prices / Demand bars / Good demand

The two diagrams above illustrate idealised market movements. In diagram A, the price of stock is falling in alignment with supply, indicated by the equal supply bars to the angle of descent. Diagram B shows the opposite; prices are rising with equal demand. Together, these images illustrate the public's perception of the market; supply and demand are matched in a simplistic manner.

If you hope to become a professional trader you must realise that the reality of the situation is *never* that straightforward. The movement of markets is based on this principle, but it does not function nearly so clearly as the example above. In order to read the market accurately, you will have to cease to view it in so simplistic a fashion.

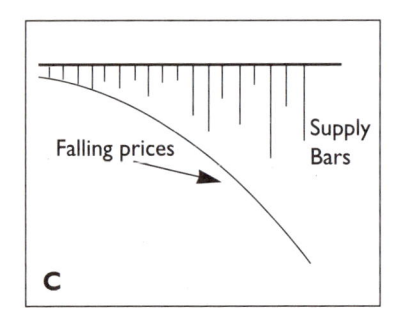

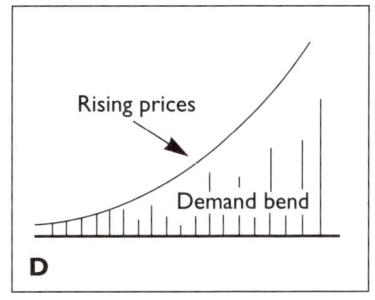

C: Falling prices / Supply Bars

D: Rising prices / Demand bend

Diagrams C and D, are a much more accurate illustration of market movement with relation to supply and demand.

Trading for a bright future

How can a market rise and fall on unsynchronised supply and demand? Let's see what the market maker would do. He has the books and can see supply and demand as it arrives, and he knows where the stops will be triggered - in other words, when the specified price of securities is reached, causing the said securities to be sold and released into the market. When stops are triggered, supply and demand are delivered very quickly.

Let's assume that I am the market maker, and I have all the information before me. XYZ stock has been stagnant for some time, but a small press announcement about it has generated interest, and I am beginning to get some demand. This increases with time, but as it was a stagnant stock I am not holding very much. Now I need it - and fast. I have the books, and I know who is holding large blocks of this stock. I know what they paid for it, and I know that they can sell it easily. I decide to order on it if the price goes below a certain level.

First, I will mark the price down on XYZ stock. Buyers will come in and purchase so I have to do this quickly. Some buy as the price falls, but I make more stock available to cater for the demand, which makes it possible for me to mark the price down even further. The buyers that bought at higher prices begin to feel uncomfortable, and telephone to place stops - arranging to sell it off at a designated price - in the event of it falling even further. Next, I mark down the price and trigger the sell stops of the large block of stock that I had sold previously. This brings a large supply into the market, which I buy up. Without delay, I mark the price of the stock back up again to stop any more selling and start to buy more stock at this price. This creates a shortage, in response to which I mark

Trading for a bright future

the prices up again. The outside traders now see that this stock has been driven down in price and has recovered sharply, and they start to buy. I continue to mark the price up as I sell the stock that I bought at much lower price, making a handsome profit.

The Circularity of Stock Movement

In an earlier section of the book, you were introduced to market basics. To acquire the ability to work it as a professional trader, you will need much more than just a superficial understanding of how it works.

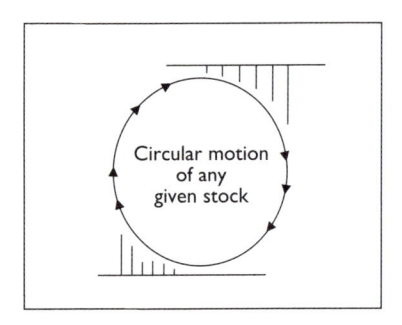

Forget the outsider's perception of the market as having peaks and troughs. Its true formation is *circular*. This circularity is inevitable because the amount of stock issued in the first place is finite. Market makers cannot simply generate fresh stock. They must work with the limited amount of material that they are presented with. The way that they work the market creates the apparent peaks and troughs that outsiders see illustrated in charts. Insiders and profitable traders view the market from a very different, and much more accurate stance.

To understand the inside view of the market, you have to remember that the quantity of any one stock is limited, and that there are two categories of stock; *floating* - that which is held by large numbers of outside traders and *fixed* - held in blocks by corporations and not likely to become available in the immediate future. Market makers can turn floating stock into fixed, by ensuring its sale, thus limiting the availability of that type of stock. They can also cause the reverse. Together, these are the actions that result in the circular motion of stock.

The cash market is contained within a constantly moving circle that is being driven and controlled by to the market makers' own advantage. They want outsiders to view the markets as random, or as a case of simple supply and demand, and thus market action is hidden from view. The market makers *simply do not want* the outsiders to see which stock is being accumulated and which is being distributed. If everybody understood the reasons behind their actions, they would lose their position of power.

Professional traders need to know some very basic information - which stocks are being accumulated, and which are being distributed. You will need to understand how and why stock is accumulated, and what the differences are between a short-term exercise - when it is hoped that a profit will be made relatively quickly - and a long term one - when more time is invested in the profit.

Long Term Accumulation

This begins with a stock that is relatively cheap at current levels, and that may have become unpopular among traders. Frequently it is also a stock that has a large floating supply. One that is often consistent with this description is a recent flotation that had great initial success, and has sound underlying value. (Floating supply is stock that is widely held by small outsider investors, both weak and strong holders).

Let's look at an example of the market in action. We'll assume that XYZ stock has been floated and purchased widely by both strong and weak holders. Some gains have been made, and outsiders have earned a little money. The market makers have noticed that each time the stock lifts a little, the outsiders sell and take their profits, thus creating a whipsaw effect. This stock will not rise significantly in value until the selling that occurs each time it lifts is halted. The only way that this will happen is if the stock is transferred from weak to strong holders. The weak holders - often under-funded, over-extended and interested in the short-term - are vulnerable and easy to exploit.

Accumulation may begin with a press announcement that mentions that certain 'types' of stock are not in fashion. When news spreads, a lot of traders will sell because of the 'bad' news. The market makers will not buy up at this point, but will start marking prices down, resulting in triggering stocks and causing yet more traders to sell. The press release now appears to have been accurate, and the papers can say, "I told you so".

If any professional body is trying to accumulate stock for a large rally, it will need to remove all the floating stock it can from the market place. If floating stock exists in large quantities, then any rally or price recuperation is in danger of being swamped. Market makers themselves cannot risk accumulating all the stock, so they use the powerful purchasing capacity of the institutions to absorb these quantities of floating stock.

Once the institutions have been persuaded to take this stock as an investment, a large block of it is removed from the marketplace, locking away the possibility of that stock suddenly being sold into a rising market, and weakening or destroying the rally. Now, the market makers, having accumulated a final block of stock themselves, release some positive news and start to mark up the price. The market makers are *always* in a position of power, in possession of all the information they need for organising these events to take place. It is this sort of manipulation that prevents weak holders from making money on the markets.

Short-Term Accumulation

Short-term accumulation occurs during ordinary market days, when market makers acquire stock quickly to mark it up in price and sell it soon afterwards at a profit.

The 'Downside' - what does the Market Maker do when there is Little or No Demand for a Stock?

Imagine that a market maker has the same stock that we already discussed - 'XYZ' on his books - valued at one pound sterling. But this time, there is little or no demand for it. To get rid of the stock, the market maker has a number of options. He can start to sell it off, but if there is no demand, the price will fall, as it is exceeded by the supply, and a loss will be made.

Another way forward is to create an artificial demand. This can be done by generating interest in the stock by marking the price up and down - activity always draws attention. Each time the price lifts a little, the market maker will sell into the rise, so every share sold over the average cost of one pound lowers the cost of the remaining shares. This has the benefit of enabling the market maker to sell at a lower price and still make a profit.

Eventually he will unload the unpopular stock, and replace it with good, tradable stock. At the same time, he is selling cheap call options in the knowledge that there is no demand and that these options will expire as worthless. Opportunities can also be generated for the market maker in the futures market.

The Reality of Market Activity.

These diagrams provide a simplified version of market activity, illustrating the movement of three stocks.

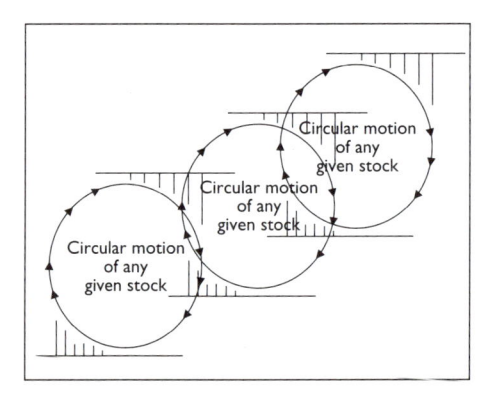

In this diagram, you can see how the cash market, containing multiple stock, advances.

In the second one, you can see the decline of the cash market containing multiple stocks.

Trading for a bright future

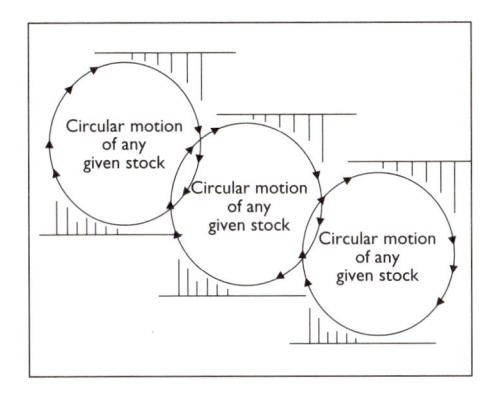

Needless to say, in a real market things are much more complex - for example, in the FTSE 100 index there are 100 moving stocks. Some are in the full flow of the upwardly moving circle, while others are moving downwards. As if that were not complicated enough, there are two further variables that must be understood in order to read the market, the movement of circles within circles and the 'elastic' nature of the movement of any one stock.

The Complex Nature of Stock Movement

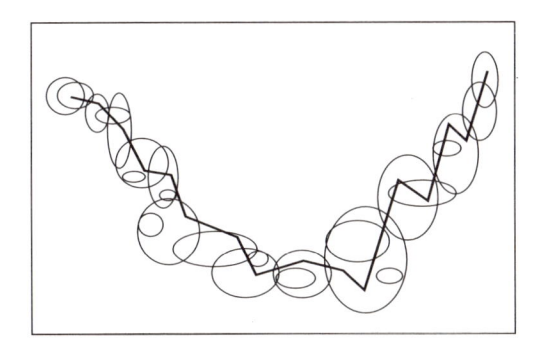

This 'circles within circles' image is a realistic map of price movement, accumulation and distribution in the market. Each circle represents a process of rising and falling prices of the stock in question and the red line represents a chart

Trading for a bright future

illustration of market activity. Remember that there are many people involved at *every level* of stock distribution and movement. The briefest of glances at this diagram is enough to understand why it is very difficult to read the market, but, to be optimistic, acknowledging the difficulties is an important step towards understanding. Don't let yourself be intimidated, even a seasoned trader can be confused at times. Learn how to read the market, and also how to know when to walk away, a very important skill if you are to retain your profits!

The Elastic Nature of Stock Movement

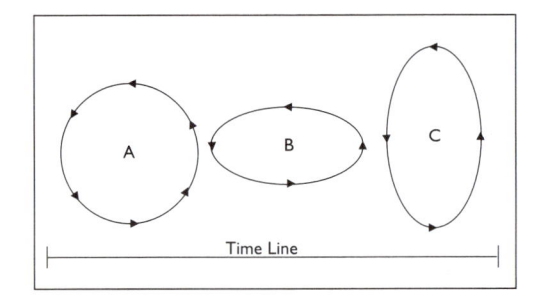

In the illustration above, A represents a circle of stock turnover. The acts of buying and selling the stock are taking place in a systematic buy, sell, buy mode, demonstrated by the regular shape of the diagram. In example B, the loop has been elongated by time, and the price has a less travelled price range than example A - in other words, the difference between the lowest and highest price in the time illustrated is smaller. The shape also indicates that the stock was purchased over a longer time period. The stock then started on a slow rise, which then ran into selling over a longer time period, before returning to the buying area. Example C has depth, indicating a wide price range, but over a shorter time period, with a fast rise in prices, a short selling period and a fast fall.

What does this imply in the real world of market activity? In the first example (A), there is a constant turnover of stock, so what we are seeing is accumulation and distribution on a relatively steady basis. The market makers are making money from the bid and ask prices - just as one would expect.

In the second example (B), the accumulation of stock takes place over a longer time period. This may or may not be long-term accumulation; perhaps it is nothing more than simple rotation of stock between buyers and sellers. The only time that we can take an educated view of the activities during this period is when the stock begins to move away from the flat area, indicating the time period during which the price neither rises nor falls. If it is genuine stock accumulation, we can expect to see a long and steady rise in value. If it is merely rotation, we can expect to witness a short rise, and then some selling off as the buyers lose interest in an immobile stock.

In the last example (C), we can see that the stock spends a short period in an accumulation phase at the bottom, a fast rise and a sell-off followed by a sharp fall.

Trading for a bright future

Market Behaviour in Real Situations

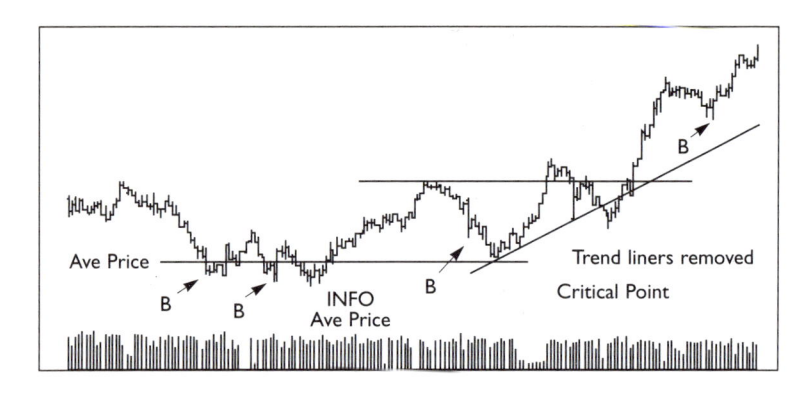

Using this diagram as our guide, let's examine how the market behaviour I have just described functions in real cash market situations.

The points indicated in the diagram at 'B' illustrate when purchases were made. These were carried out in a deceptive manner, occurring during market falls - a time when outsiders tend to sell because of their impartial understanding of market activity.

While all the outsiders were selling, the insiders - market makers and professional traders- were buying up. The indicator at 'Info. Ave. Price' (Information about the average price) shows the point at which the level-headed trader is acquiring information about the average cost price of all the purchases that the professionals are making.

Meanwhile, the market was driven down to remove stops that were just below the second 'B' from the left, causing the outside holders to sell stock[11] into the market. This helps the professionals, in that the last remaining stock is made available for purchase. At this point,

---

[11] Here, the term 'stock' is used to refer to both futures and normal equities.

Trading for a bright future

the market recovers quickly and is lifted above the average price line, placing the professional money in safe territory. Insiders are not facing a loss.

What exactly has happened? The professional market has bought heavily in the knowledge that there was underlying strength in the cash market. The price is now above their average cost and they have no cause for concern. Anything that is now sold off to the outsiders shows a handsome profit.

The market then rises steadily and consistently from the sale of stock index constituents to an outside public. At this time, the outsiders are making money because the stock is rising, and so are the professionals, as they have a willing public to which they can sell. In the final flurry of selling to outsiders, the market 'gaps up' or takes a sudden leap in perceived or actual value and there is a sell-off.

The market makers and the professional money have sold all the stock that they purchased some time ago. Now they need more stock, and the only way to get it is to buy it back. Of course, if they want to make a profit, they can't buy it back at the same high price at which they sold it some time ago; they need to buy it at the lowest average price possible.

The market is marked down, which causes panic amongst the outsiders who bought it on the rise. Prices reach the designated stops, causing the stock to become available for purchase, but the professional money does not yet step in and buy it. Finally, at the third 'B', many stops are triggered, as stock reaches its stop price, or that at which the trader has decided to sell in an effort to minimise loss should its value decline, and consequently, the market falls rapidly. As the price of stock falls, the professional money is discreetly buying it up - don't forget that these are the people with inside information, those who know the underlying strengths and weaknesses of the market.

At the same time, some buying of stock on the part of the traders occurs, forcing the price to lift a little. But the professional money knows that stock is available at cheaper prices. The market starts to move lower, until the price reaches exactly the average price paid for it earlier by the professional money. Heavy buying occurs and the market heads into a settled bull phase, the prevailing belief being that there is about to be a rise in the market in general or in a part of it. Stock is sold once again to the outside market, and again there is a sell off and then a drive down. By now, some outsiders, including some quite big trend traders, understand what is going on, and they decide to buy stock and hold it. The market is then brought down to break a trend pattern, removing trend traders from their long positions. At that stage, the market develops into a rise and fall pattern of acceleration.

•

Are you asking yourself how you can ever hope to become a strong holder without being privy to the financial muscle or information that the market makers have? As a trader you are, by definition, on the outside of the market in comparison to the market maker. To make progress you have to use the best tools at your disposal. In short, your brain, and your knowledge of how market makers function.

To trade like a professional you have to be able to *think the way the market makers do*, to be able to look at the market from the inside, and to disregard the *apparent* dynamics of the market, which attract most peoples' attention and cause many traders to make serious mistakes. You must learn to understand exactly how one particular group of traders act and react to market conditions. This will give you a depth of insight comparable to that of the market-makers.market from the inside, and to disregard the *apparent* dynamics of the market, which attract most peoples' attention and cause many traders to make serious mistakes. You must learn to understand exactly how one particular group of traders act and react to market conditions. This will give you a depth of insight comparable to that of the market-makers.

Trading for a bright future

Trading for a bright future

CHAPTER NINE

Introducing the Bright Futures Strategy

The strategy known as 'Bright Futures' is all about understanding the *reasons behind* market activity and volume; recognising them for the births and deaths of the belief structures that they are. It is also about understanding oneself, and becoming enabled to make trading decisions based on intellectually rather than emotionally derived information.

In order to fully understand the Bright Futures strategy, you will need to know what a belief structure is and how its life cycle functions. To appreciate the interpretations offered here, it is also important that you start to examine your own beliefs about certain aspects of your life.

All of us hold beliefs about ourselves, others and everything around us. These dictate our daily actions to a considerable extent. Generally speaking, we will only carry out a task that contains an element of risk if we believe that we are able to.

Imagine that there is two inch wide plank fifty feet high that spans two buildings. You need to get from one building to another. As you look down, the possibility of falling will cause you to question your belief that you are able to make it across. The very same plank on the ground will not, of course, threaten your belief in your ability to succeed in crossing.

Traders should always bear in mind that it is *only possible to hold one belief about a particular concept at any one time*. In the case of the example of the plank, one cannot believe that it is possible to make it across the plank and at the same time believe that it is not.

How does all this relate to the market? To put it simply, one cannot believe that the market will go up and at the same time believe it will go down.

Some traders may argue that they have no belief about future market direction. While this seems possible, a belief about future market direction is inevitably born at some point. When it occurs, the trader may be ready to take a trade that is consistent with his belief.

Once the trade has been placed, his belief is suddenly reinforced to the point that all other possible outcomes are rejected. The further the market moves in the anticipated direction, the stronger and stronger the trader's belief will become. This process may be referred to as 'birth of a belief structure'. The trader is very vulnerable at this time, as irrationality can take over, and indicators that show the end of the market direction may be overlooked.

Attachment to a belief structure is completely natural - and it is fully understood and exploited by the market makers.

Once you have started mapping the market in terms of belief structures rather than price you will be able to understand market activity from the same perspective as the market maker. Price is not the real issue. Traders who concentrate on price are unable to give the currently held belief structures the necessary attention.

Trading for a bright future

Nothing lasts forever, and belief structures are particularly fickle! In order for a new belief to be born the previously held one must be changed. This process is always a painful experience, because one has to 'cut the umbilical cord' of the currently held belief. In trading, losses are often inevitable at this point. The unpleasant experience of taking a loss creates a subconscious association in the trader's mind between changing a belief and pain or stress, seriously affecting future trading decisions.

Understanding Market Beliefs

The revelation of the astonishing degree of consistency in belief structures came to me during a live trading course that I conducted some time ago. To test the 'pain threshold' of a group of students holding losing positions, I performed a simple exercise. Each person marked the results of flipping a coin a hundred times on a sheet of graph paper. The number of flips was plotted on the X axis, while the Y axis indicated whether a tail or a head had come up. Each time a head came up, the students marked a cross one box higher and vice versa for a tail.

Participants were also asked to mark the point on their chart where they started to *believe* that the point would be above or below the starting point after the hundred throws were completed. If the 'market' subsequently moved against them, they were also asked to mark the plot at the point where they changed their mind about the final result.

I deliberately misrepresented the results so that the plot was well above the starting point after about fifty throws. Once participants had committed themselves to the belief that the 'market' would finish above the starting point,

Trading for a bright future

I began to manipulate the results in the opposite direction.

The alternation between discomfort when the position moved against them and relief when a few heads were called was palpable. But the really astonishing thing was that, although the students were unable to see each others' charts, they were all remarkably similar. The points at which participants marked their belief that the result would finish above the line and where they changed their minds were virtually identical. That made it clear that the way in which traders' belief structures change over time and price could be used in formulating an efficient trading technique.

The Mechanics of The Bright Futures Strategy

BF Day Strategies

The **set-up day** is a day when all the price action falls within the price range of the previous day, indicating an appropriate point for the implementation of the *Bright Futures Strategy*. The next day is termed the **Bright Futures day.** Trading begins at this point, with the trader looking for a substantial move in either direction from the mid point of the set-up day bar. It is vital to trade with the trend.

A set-up day is illustrated graphically as an 'inside bar' - the lines which indicate price action are clearly drawn within the parameters of the previous day's bar. There are two basic types. The first is a normal set-up day that can be expected to trade over a period of three days. The second is a set-up day that forms with a higher volume

Trading for a bright future

content than the previous day. The latter case contains a *greater number of beliefs* about the future price than that of the preceding bar.

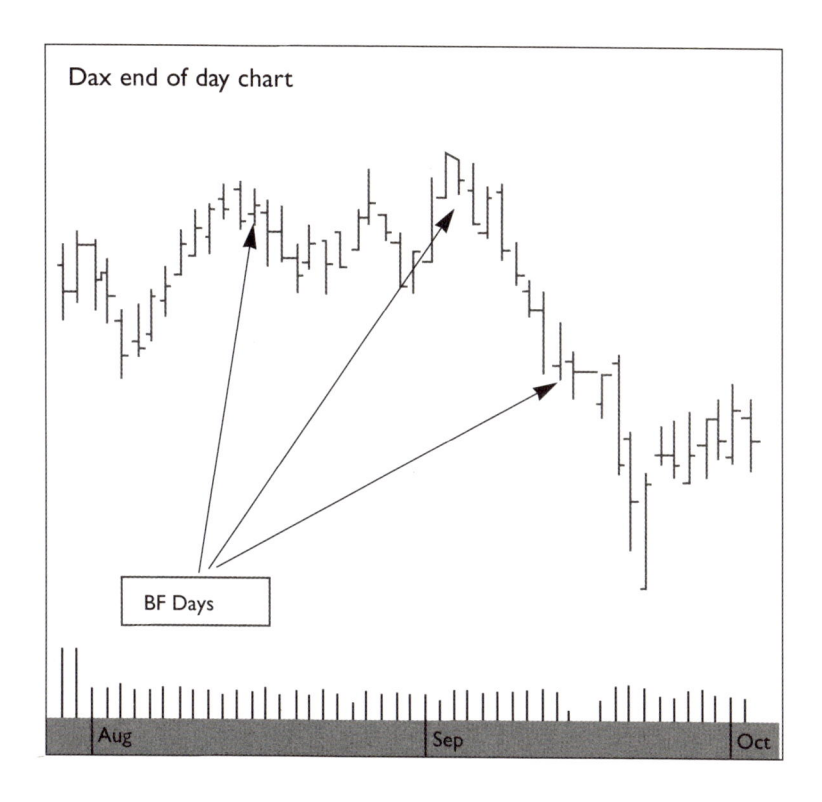

[Dax end of day chart showing BF Days from Aug to Oct]

The arrow points on the diagram above indicate inside day bars. As you can see, these days are fairly infrequent. Statistically, they only occur two or three times a month in any market. This very infrequency is what makes them so noteworthy. Remember that within the Bright Futures Strategy what they represent are *a compression of belief structures, not mere market activity.*

I refer to days which fall outside the Bright Futures strategy as 'white days'. The best that these days can offer is a 50/50 chance of winning. As trading is a negative sum gain, these odds are unacceptable and trading in such circumstances is to be avoided.

To prepare for trading on a Bright Futures day, you need to calculate the *mid price of the set-up bar* and also calculate a buy line and a sell line. The buy and sell points (DAX example) should be a minimum of 15 points on either side of the mid line price. This gives us a 30-point range between the buy and sell lines. There is no way of knowing where the market will open in relation to the mid line price, but this is not a major concern as several tools are available to select a low risk entry point. Bear the concepts of belief structures and their boundaries in mind.

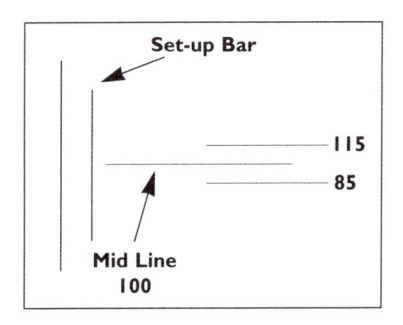

```
        Set-up Bar
    ←
    |
    |———————— 115
    |
    |———————— 85
    ↑
    Mid Line
    100
```

The underlying principle at work is that if the market is *below* the mid line price then it will have *inherent weakness*. If it is *above* the midline price then there is *inherent strength*.

The Bright Futures strategy is based upon the fact that there has been a tighter trading range than the previous day, revealing that the belief structures of the market have become compressed.

As traders tend to place stops at the extremes of their belief structures, it is at these points that they will either be removed from the market or join in the market in the opposite direction from their original beliefs.

Trading for a bright future

Because of the tight containment on a Bright Futures day we can expect to see the collapse of belief structures on a reasonably large scale with the addition of new belief structures forming. Remember that to reverse the direction of the market, a corresponding collapse and birth in the new direction are necessary. The collapse of sufficient numbers of belief structures gives the market momentum and distance of movement. In these circumstances, the market can be traded on the basis of holding one's position until it has moved a good distance from the Bright Futures mid line.

The Components of the Bright Futures Strategy

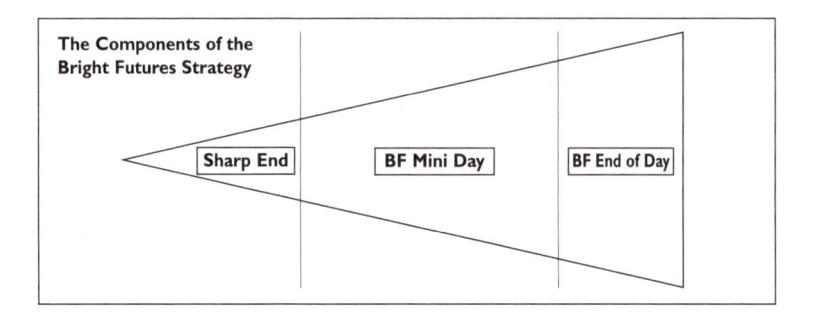

[Diagram: The Components of the Bright Futures Strategy — a horizontal triangle/wedge expanding from left to right, with three labelled boxes along the horizontal axis: "Sharp End" (left), "BF Mini Day" (middle), "BF End of Day" (right).]

The Bright Futures Strategy consists of three components. Each of these is linked to the next, while still useful as a separate strategy which may be used in trading. The strategy is flexible, and each trader can adapt it to his own requirements, personality and situation.

The trading period for the use of the Bright Futures strategy is very clear. The starting point is the 'set-up day', when one observes certain market characteristics indicating a favourable climate for trading with the Bright Futures strategy. The trading period begins the subsequent

Trading for a bright future

day, and continues for a period of three days. Day one is referred to as 'BF day', day two 'BF+1' and day three 'BF+2'. On day one significant market trends are expected to develop with substantial points on offer.

In the diagram above, the point referred to as the 'sharp end' illustrates the use of the Bright Futures Strategy with a tick chart. As each tick indicates a distinct market action, information is undistorted by being compressed into a bar.

A mini-BF day demonstrates all the same indicators as a BF day, but appears in a ten minute chart rather than a day chart. It can be used to gain a foothold in the market by identifying areas of conflicting belief structures. Once identified, the BF trader then turns to the 'sharp end' to gain an entry point into the market.

The term 'end of day' refers, simply, to the close of a day's trading. The information obtained from an end of day chart is necessary in making trading decisions.

In trading with the Bright Futures strategy, I have learned to use a 'three to one rule'. In short, *never enter the market unless you expect to take points three times to the value of your stop*. On a BF day we expect to take in excess of 90 points (if we use the DAX as our model). Thus one can enter under as a fixed rule with a 30-point stop.

On a BF day that does not fall within the fixed rule criteria, one does not expect to take excessive of points as in both these instances part of the move has already taken place. The three to one rule is still valid, because using a predefined entry strategy, one should always be able to enter the market with a fairly tight stop.

The identification of belief boundaries is a vital component of trading with the Bright Futures strategy. These occur because of traders' commitments to a position

Trading for a bright future

and to what can be termed a 'belief change zone' through which they will travel before changing their position, whether voluntarily or not.

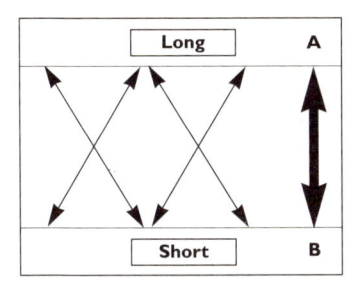

Anywhere between points A and B in the illustration above, traders will sit out a trade. These are big profit areas for market makers for the simple reason that traders place stops at extremes of their belief boundaries.

How can you locate these boundaries and then use them for trading profits? Quite easily. One of the most important aspects of trading around belief structure boundaries is the clear identification of them. They are signalled by the presence of market energy that is *much greater than that of normal market activity*. The volume histogram chart shown below delivers this information.[12]

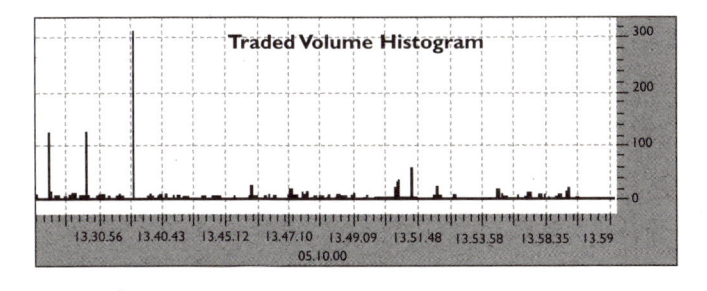

---

[12] Many software packages enable the user to alter the scaling of this window and how the data is supplied. For instance, a volume activity of 15 can be multiplied up to read as 150 and, similarly, activity of 150 can show up as 1,500. It is not important what scale you use, so long as you stick to that one scale relative to the instrument that you are trading.

Trading Beliefs

Let's examine some real examples of how belief moves the market. The charts that I use to illustrate the text show real-life belief structures in the German DAX market, and have been chosen from a very typical market day.

Chart One

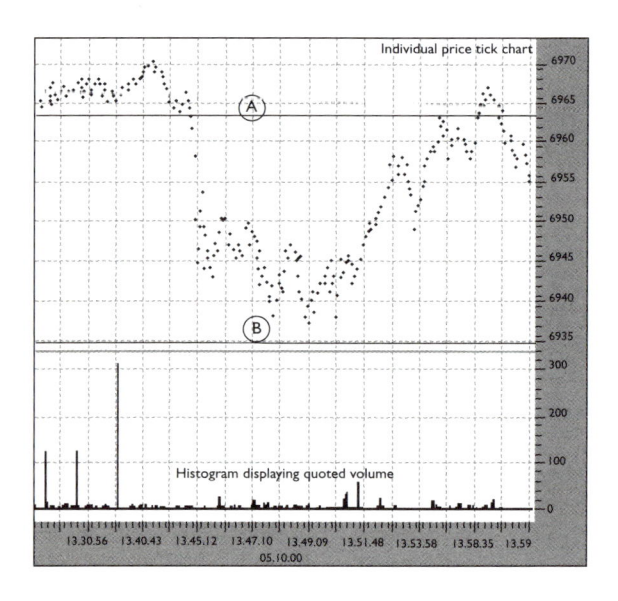

On the right of this chart there is a scale showing prices from 6935-6970 and another of 0-300 showing the amount of quoted volume. The two broken lines are drawn at prices where a sudden and very high level of trader activity took place. In other words, a significant number of traders developed a *strong enough belief about the value of future prices* to justify entering the market at the indicated points. You must understand that not every trader had the same belief at these points/prices. Clearly, if 500 traders had all suddenly sold the market generating

Trading for a bright future

this large volume bar the market would not have maintained stability for long enough to allow you to join them.

The chart illustrates a large volume of traders entering the market with *conflicting* beliefs about the value of the future price. It is this conflict of belief that can be used to generate trading profits.

In order for a market to move away from this area of high activity there must be an imbalance of buyers and sellers. If there are more sellers than buyers the price will start to move down. If there are more buyers than sellers the price will start to move up.

Belief Chart One shows that the sellers quickly overtook the buyers and the prices fell rapidly. However, at point B on the chart there was another area of conflicting beliefs that took place earlier in the day as indicated in Belief Chart Two. *(overleaf)*

Belief Chart Two

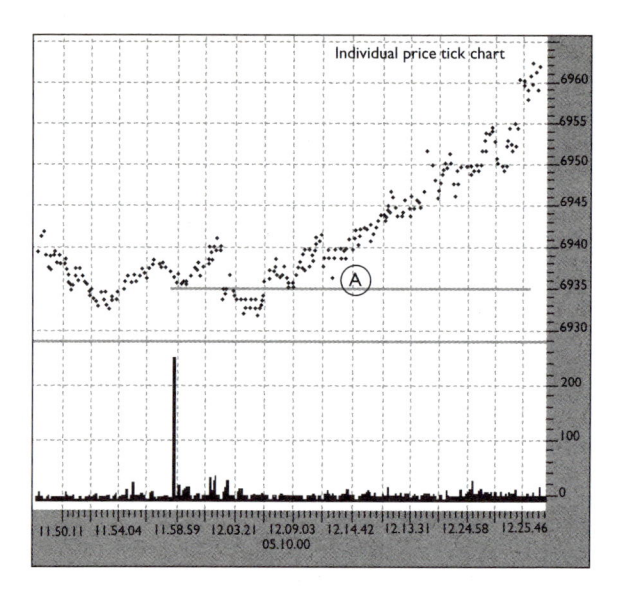

If you note the time at the bottom edge of this chart, you will see that the high trader activity took place at 11:59 am, when the price was around 6935. You will also note that the market moves swiftly away from this area.

In brief, the buyers overtook the sellers and the result was a clean up move in the market. Because of the high activity and knowledge of the underlying strength/weakness of the market, an excellent low risk entry point was presented later on into the trading day as shown in Belief Chart Four *(see page 119)*.

Belief Chart One

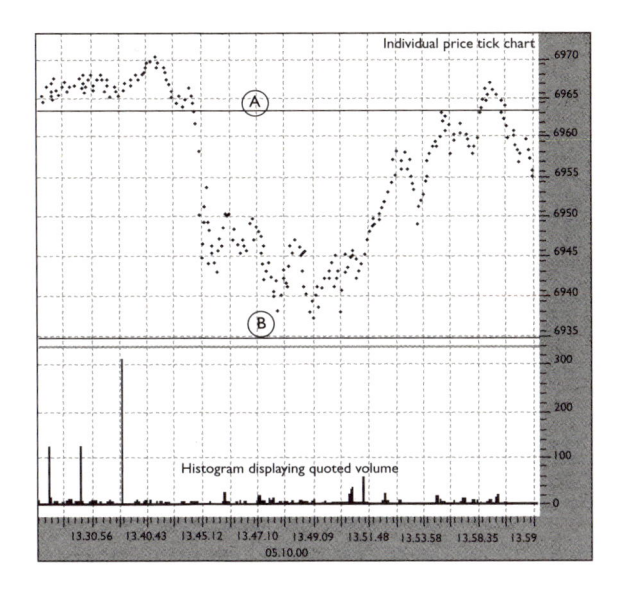

Returning to Belief Chart One, now illustrating activity at around 13:35p.m., one can see another injection of high trader activity. The market falls away, but encounters the high trader activity area (representing currently held beliefs) that occurred approximately 90 minutes earlier. This is indicated by the lower broken line at point B. As a result of these currently held beliefs - illustrated on the chart at around 6935 - the market loses its downward momentum and encounters the manifestation of a set of beliefs that it has underlying strength - namely, orders placed by traders. We are now faced with two boundary markers that are approximately 30 points apart (remember the test that I carried out, explained earlier?).

Belief Chart Three

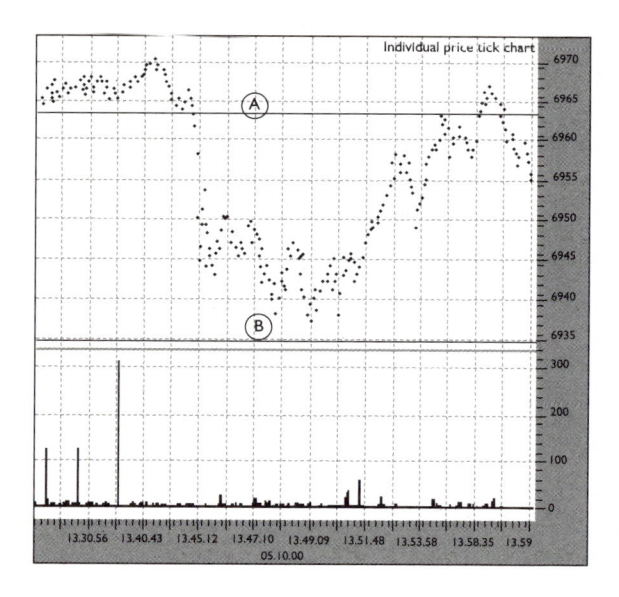

In the diagram above, one can see the development of a conflicting set of belief structures - and another potential profit opportunity. Always bear in mind that *price is not the issue.*

What one sees are two opposing forces and there will be a victor to reap the rewards. The price moves towards the top boundary line and breaks through, causing the trader to place a buy order just above the top at 6969/70. The market fails to reach this price again so he is not filled. Then the market starts to 'rebound', moving down from the top boundary. At this point all the trader should look for is a break out of this compression area. The direction of the break out does not have implications from the point of view of gaining a profit.

Belief Chart Four

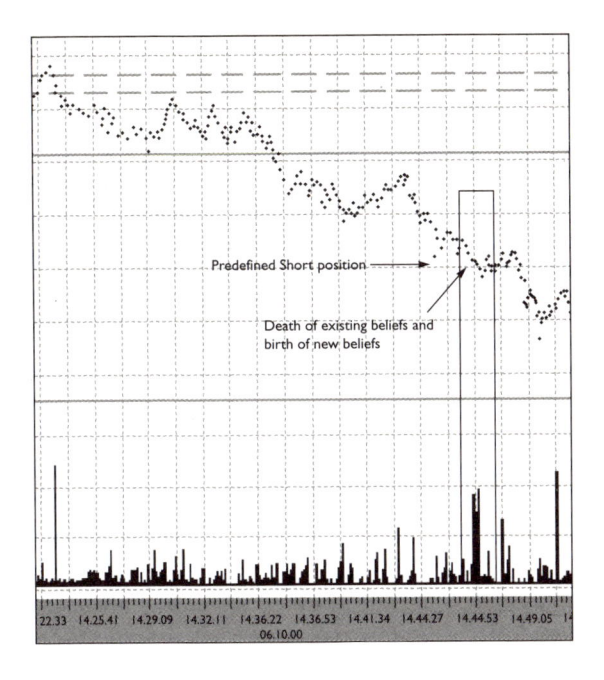

The two boundaries are now shown on Belief Chart Four by the two sets of horizontal dashed lines.

Many traders, on seeing the price move away from the area marked with a B in Belief Chart Three, will have bought into the market and placed stops around this area. Here, in Belief Chart Four the market breaks through an area of beliefs in the strength of the market (shown by the lower dotted line). In doing so, the stops of the traders (mentioned earlier) who hold this belief are encountered.

This point is clearly marked by the high activity indicated by the volume bars. The buy stops are quickly absorbed and the result is a further fall in prices. A pre-defined exit on a limit order at 6895 would give the trader using the Bright Futures strategy a 30 point profit. The birth, challenge, death and then re-birth of belief structures are what drive the market in any given direction at any given time.[13]

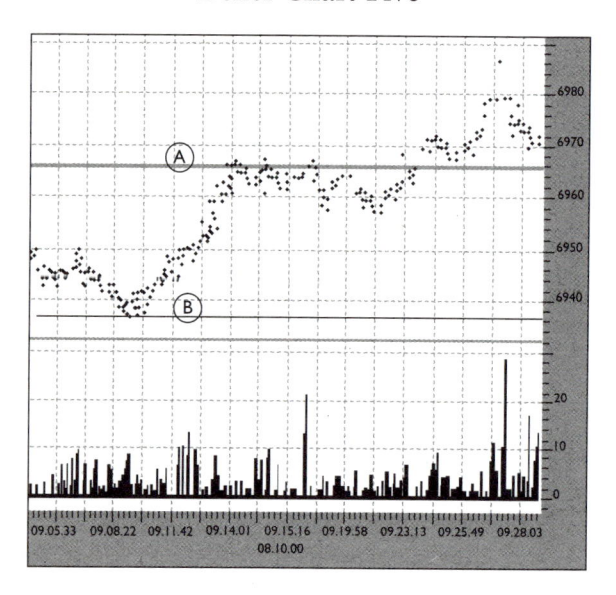

Belief Chart Five

The horizontal lines at points A and B are those from the previous day carried forward. The market breaks to the up side of the belief boundary. So traders who traded this on the break out are quickly in the money. But where is the energy? It has been dissipated for the upside because of the break to the low side the day before, seen on the previous chart.

---

[13] The only reason this trade would be taken is because of the contained energy; it is this energy that gives us the opportunity to take sufficient points out of the market to justify our risk reward ratio. Many traders will enter the market on simply break-outs of local tops and bottoms. This is not a reliable technique, as unless there is energy contained within the market at the point of break-out, the market is unlikely to go very far before a retrace to the area where stops will be placed. Belief Chart Five, is an example of this.

Belief Chart Six

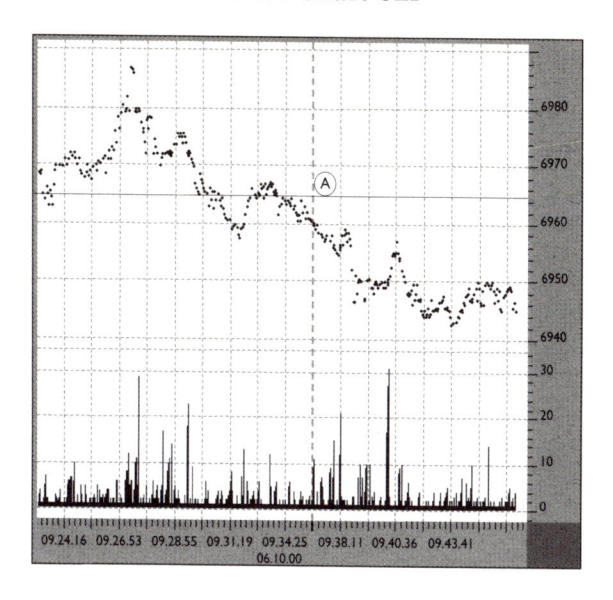

This chart depicts a development of the previous one. Clearly, belief in the market was not strong enough to take it higher. The break to the low side on the previous day had the effect of stopping out those who believed in higher prices. *Their belief structure was destroyed, while those to the short side became reinforced.*

The most important lesson to remember here is that there must be energy to warrant taking a trading position. If energy is not present, a trade should never be taken. Trading on the mere hope that a market will break a top or bottom and then continue in that direction is a sure way to erode your account.

Bright Futures Trading
Three Scenarios

There are three ways in which to trade on a BF day, which will be referred to in the text as scenarios one, two and three.

Scenario One

Scenario one is a fixed system method used when the market opens close to or within the 30-point range that has already been calculated. In other words, it is only possible when the market opens *close to or within the plus or minus 15 points* calculated from the centre line. The strategy invoked is simply to buy or sell the market as it passes through either boundary. Once the trader has received a fill-back, a stop of some thirty points needs to be placed at the other boundary price.[14]

The trader's position should now be held until a profit target of 90 or more points has been reached. The only time the stop should be moved on a day in which a fixed system method is being implemented is when a top or bottom is breached. It should then be moved to the last relevant top or bottom, depending on whether the trader is in a long or short position. This stop moving should be carried out using a time frame chart of not less than 10 minutes. Let's examine how this works in practice, using the diagram on the facing page as our guide.

---

[14] This is the only time I advocate a fixed stop based on a numerical calculation.

Trading for a bright future

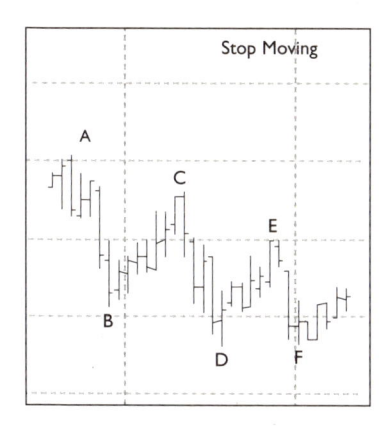

Assume that the trader sold the market at point A. As it moved towards Point B, many traders were tempted to move stops to lock in a profit or limit their loss. On a BF day *and only on a BF day*, the stop strategy is as follows. First, the trade is given some 'breathing space'. Then, as you can see, the market moves, favourably for the trader using the Bright Futures strategy, towards Point B. The BF trader then waits for Point B to be broken on the down side before moving his stop to point C. Then he waits for Point D to be broken on the down side before moving his stop to position E. In this example, point D was not broken until later in the day. By holding a position on a BF day to a targeted exit point the trader can expect to gain substantial points. Do not forget that the trade was started on a BF day with a 30 point stop. The trader must have a target exit of at least 90 points. This is sometimes referred to in the market as the 'risk reward ratio'. That is, how many points you put at risk for however many points of potential reward. The risk reward here is 1:3.

Trading for a bright future

Scenario Two

Assume that the market opens some 60 points above the mid line price (indicating strength), and the trader is not offered an opportunity to trade using a fixed system method. At this point he must turn to a tick chart to gain an advantageous entry point. Remember that the odds are still stacked in his favour, as he is only interested in the long side of the market.

The tick chart is used to identify a specific type of price movement, best explained as a clean move away from a specific area with interest. Let's take a look at a visual representation of this phenomenon.

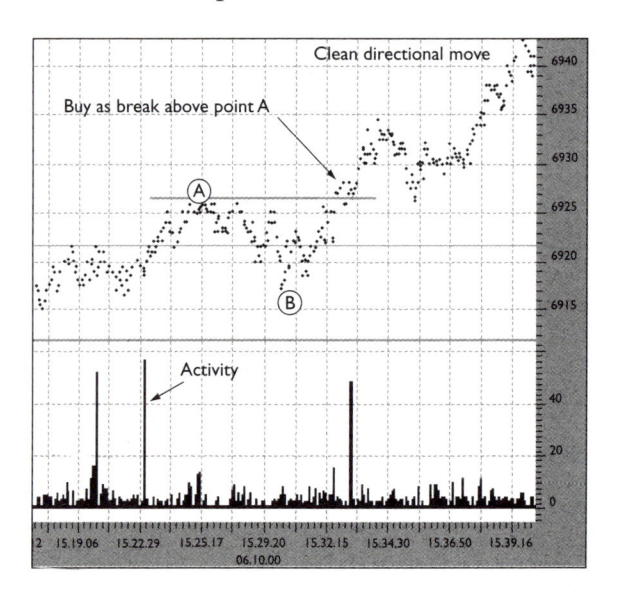

The key component here is that point B is of no interest to the BF trader, as it is anticipated that the market will move up. This market should only be entered if the top at point A is broken through. One benefit of entering the market in this manner is that if the market does not break

Trading for a bright future

the top at point A, the BF trader will not be filled, and not long in the market. The high activity bar gives us further evidence of a significant directional move. In summary, the decision making process that is carried out here incorporates; interest exclusively in the long side of the market, the sudden entry of a significant amount of trader activity, the forming of a top which pinpoints an appropriate entry point, and the expectation of a move of sufficient size to enable the taking of a profit.

Scenario Three

In this scenario, the BF day has opened with a large gap up or gap down and exhausted the move that was due to take place. This exhaustion will take place at around one hundred points from the BF midline price on the set up day on the German DAX index as it currently trades. Once this has happened, it is very likely that the market will drift back towards the mid line price. Trading in this situation is known as **exhaustion trading**. To gain a low risk entry point one should use a tick chart.

The entry strategy in this scenario is the same as that employed in the previous one. Of course, in this case the market has gapped up or down thereby literally exhausting any potential move in that direction. The BF trader trades in the direction of the drift back towards the BF line.

Stop Strategies

The stop strategies that should be used on BF days depend upon which scenario pertains when the trader enters the

Trading for a bright future

market.

Scenario one, initiating a trade under fixed system conditions with the market opening close to the mid line price and then breaking though is traded using the simple stop strategy of selecting tops or bottoms in, for example, a 10 minute chart.

The stop strategy for scenario two is different because, whereas under fixed system conditions the initial stop would be 30 points (the difference between the buy and sell line as calculated from the mid line price), in these conditions the trader is looking at the clean move away, followed by the location of his stop in the area from where the clean move started.

In the case of scenario three, the same chart that we used earlier to identify the clean move away can also be employed in identifying where the stop should be located.

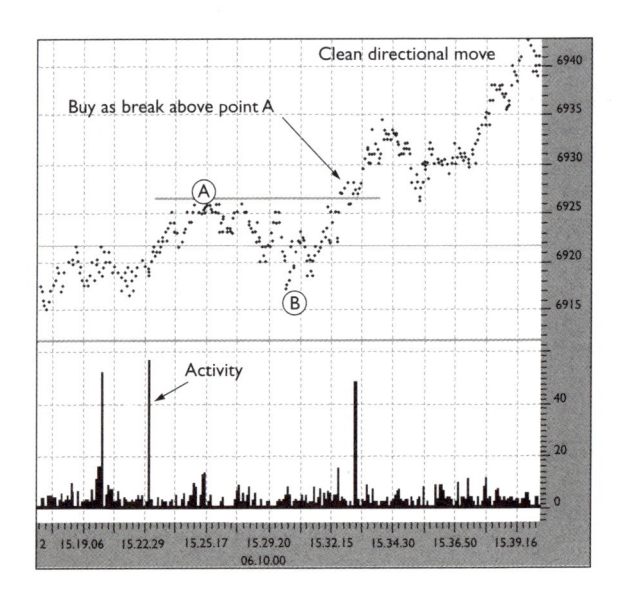

Trading for a bright future

Once the BF trader is filled long at point A, point B becomes an excellent stop area for two reasons. First, that the clean move away from point B occurred because of the high activity bar. Once the market went above point A there is confirmation that the high activity bar was in line with the belief of an upward moving market. It can, then, be reasonably assumed that to go below point B after breaking above point A would mean that the predominant belief structures would have to be broken. If this were to happen, the market would no longer hold interest for the BF trader.

The benefits of mastering this stop strategy is that the trader enters the market at a time when there is high activity, suggesting that the market will move a sufficient distance to warrant taking the trade. The stop is also very close to your entry position, minimising risk.

Trading BF +1 and BF +2

The days thus described can be traded within the Bright Futures trading strategy, but a different set of criteria needs to be employed.

The criterion for entry is exactly the same as that used for trading scenario two, *(shown on 124 page)*. This is, of course, trading in one direction only on the basis of where the market is in relation to the mid line price of the set-up day. The market is only entered when there is sufficient activity to suggest that it will travel far enough to fall within your risk consideration. The trader will exit from the market at a well-defined point derived from the employment of the three to one rule.

Trading for a bright future

•

The examples that I have chosen to explain the Bright Futures strategy have largely been taken from the DAX market - this is simply because this is the market that I trade, and not because it is the only market that can be traded using the techniques that I have described.

The Bright Futures strategy is not based solely on mathematical formula - it is a living, breathing strategy that takes into account the natural rhythms of the market. Because of this underlying factor, the strategy can be applied to any instrument that offers you the same information that the DAX provides, can be plotted on a tick chart, and is sufficiently mobile to warrant trading it.

Traders who recognise the Bright Futures strategy as an important trading tool are ensuring that the odds are very much in their favour. It is not, however, a *magic* formula. Patience, an investment of time and adaptation of the strategy to one's own circumstances are all necessary.

The degree to which the Bright Futures strategy can be successfully applied is clearly illustrated in the improved trading results of traders introduced to the technique during the live trading courses I conduct. Typically, these traders were up considerably - from 75 to 150 points. In their own words, some of my former pupils describe recent trading successes:

Saad Ali (with perhaps a little *too* much enthusiasm):
Just wanted to let you know that, what I learnt from you at your course really paid off this morning. It was only by chance that I looked at Friday's Daily Dax this morning about 1 a.m. and guess what - a BF set-up!!! Thanks to

Trading for a bright future

you I took 90 points from the market with stops as you directed, (by way of spread betting). I bet using a stake of £50.00 per point. WOW!!! and thank you. Martin, if you were a woman I would definitely date you. Too bad you're married!

Henri Jaume:
Your system bloody well works!
By the way, took over 100 points last week. Hope you're in the best of health. Cheers. H.

Ian Rogers:
I managed to trade the BF day this morning, gaining 77.5 points before being stopped out sold at 6503.5 at 9.07

John Birbeck:
Thought about entering 6480 Waited for confirmation, entered 6470 moved stop to 6440. Missed the bottom (meetings bloody meetings!.) Exit at 6415.
Only 55 points, but I knew it was going that way!

Pam Munro:
I couldn't resist the opportunity to trade for real today and made 52 points - not bad for a first day. I got in late (at 6478) and didn't think it would go below 6400 so I was stopped out at 6426.
It just goes to prove that it isn't just a man's world but also that you can start from scratch.

Mark Young:
Well that was pretty impressive. I went short exactly where I was supposed to go short, protected myself with a stop

30 points north. I then saw the market drop to the target of 6405, fill one contract (presumably yours), bounce and then fill another.

It won't surprise you to learn that I thought it would go further, which is what I did on the course. I hung on and was wrong - again! Anyway, I did close for a pretty decent 69 points - not as good as 90, but better than anything I did before coming to see you.

So, whilst I am fairly pleased at the result, I am dissatisfied with myself. It doesn't help that I have just seen the market drop again (as I type) to 6383, as, in a way and in this instance, my sentiments were right.

I had Michael chortling on the phone - delighted to have got his 90 points, and Eric phoned to say that Charlie did the same. So their school reports will read 'Excellent', whereas mine will say 'Could do better'. Anyway, 69 points is not a bad birthday present to myself.

Henri Jaume:
Hi again. 74 points from Dax today. Would have had 90 if I had entered at 95 but wanted to be sure as market crossed the average so entered at 93. Exited at 19 after market hit 05 (2 above my exit) and retraced.

The above emails were all received on the same day and collectively resulted in over 1,000 points being taken from the Dax. While these results are impressive they are, nonetheless, what I expect from my students. That said, only with will, diligence and hard work can they achieve the levels of success that they do. For that I wholeheartedly congratulate them.

CHAPTER TEN

A Deeper Understanding of Market Trends

Market trends are, simply, the current general directions of movement of rates or prices in the market. These are studied by market traders in visual form to help them make informed decisions about implementing their strategy. To make profits, one's decisions must be consistent with trends, but how can one identify the moment at which a simple market movement becomes a trend? Trends are not entirely objective, which is yet another factor signalling the great importance of designing a strategy that accommodates the many variables contained by the market and one's personal circumstances.

If your trading time frame is three months, for instance, your perspective will be very different from that of the intra-day traders. Two different traders and two different software packages may draw trends from different points and at different times, creating all sorts of potential problems in using them as part of a trading strategy. Nonetheless, they are immensely important to long-term trading success. Market makers know of the power of trend lines, and what they represent to outsiders, so they use this information to their advantage. To maximise profit potential, one needs an accurately drawn trend line based on firm substantial evidence.

Trading for a bright future

The importance of trend lines lies in the fact that they illustrate what is happening in the market *at the current time* and what is likely to happen in the future. Once true trends have been established, it becomes relatively easy to predict whether prices will be higher or lower in the future - always subject to the trend continuing.

Trend Chart One

As a trend forms, the markets settle into different phases within it. Sometimes a trend line is broken, but the market continues in the direction of the trend. At other times, the market breaks away from the trend in a strong upward move, and then starts to head back towards the trend line. Before it reaches it, however, it resumes the trend pattern. Many traders delay in joining a trend, to wait for the market to return to the base trend line. Then of course, doubt and indecision emerge as to whether the trend will hold or be broken, thus delaying market entry further. Examine the illustration of a market trend in Trend Chart One above. Is there only one trend? If there is more than one, which would you trade?

Trading for a bright future

Is the trend affected by time? Can you even assume from the above example that a trend has been established? What tactic was employed to remove a certain group of traders?

Trend Breakaways

What is a trend breakaway? To explain properly we have to return to the act of taking a trading position. The ill-informed trader assumes that because he has a mechanical trading system he is eliminating the emotional content of that trade. However, taking a trade is more complex than he thinks, and involves various elements. In the very act of taking a position he has made an emotional commitment to trade, and has created a financial involvement in further prices, implying the need, wish and desire for the trade to be profitable.

Emotions develop because the value of the trade is in the hands of a higher authority - the market. Biochemical body changes, such as an increase in heartbeat, sweating and respiration occur.

Individual emotions are especially heightened in situations where traders are in a group (I am speaking metaphorically of the collective consciousness of traders, rather than of physical groups of people). The experience of trading is more intense, as groups bond and self congratulate. Comradeship emerges as the individuals endorse other traders' decision making. In such an environment, the slightest item of supporting evidence, whether an individual remark or a news report, is immediately consumed. In all the excitement, the trader gradually loses control of his critical faculties.

Trading for a bright future

While the winning side is revelling in the evidence that appears to support its trading tactics, there are other traders, apparently on the 'wrong' side of the trend. Those on the 'right' side, in all their arrogance, will start to point out to each other just how wrong and weak the arguments of the other side are. The losing crowd is made to feel awkward and uncomfortable, and its components will huddle together, with the 'die-hards' in the middle and the weaker believers to the outside. The longer that this situation goes on, the further and further the wrong crowd is pushed from its beliefs.

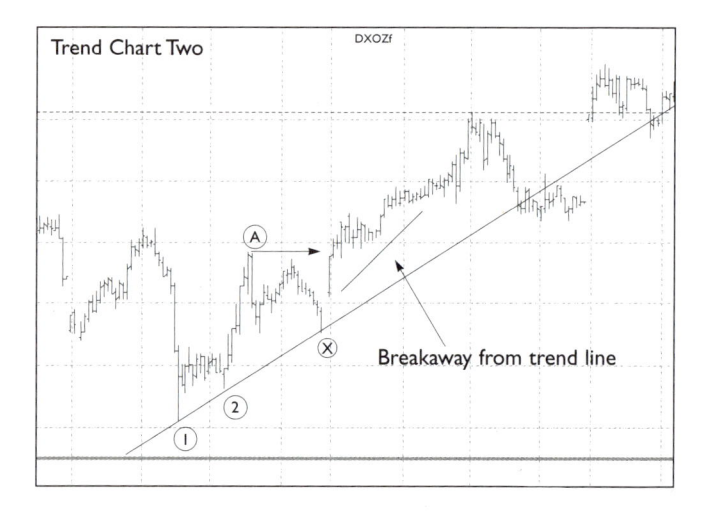

[Trend Chart Two — DXOZf; points A, X, 1, 2 labelled; arrow indicating "Breakaway from trend line"]

In Trend Chart Two, you can see points 1 and 2, from which I have drawn the trend line (please note that at the time of drawing the line, nothing illustrated beyond point 2 had yet occurred).

Although I drew the lines in at this point, I was still not entirely convinced that I had really identified a trend. I therefore, looked for a particular type of market action to endorse 1 and 2 as valid points from which to

Trading for a bright future

draw a trend line, enabling me to join the trend with confidence.[15]

In Trend Chart Two, a sharp move away from point two is apparent. Traders were encouraged to take long positions as the market started to climb away. However, the trend had not yet been truly validated, and anyone that took a position during the sharp move upward was soon subject to a retrace, taking them out of the money. The price then lifted again, offering some relief to their positions. Once again, however, it fell, taking two groups of long traders out of the money (the first group that entered on the lift from point 2 and the next, that took long positions after the first retrace had taken place). As the market got closer and closer to the trend line, the long traders placed stops, while others antici-pated that the trend would be broken, and took short positions.

Point X on the chart represents the last bar of the trading day, and both long and short traders were in limbo as the market was neither long nor short.

The following morning, the market opened above the trend line and climbed a steady 150 points with practically no retrace to challenge a stop. Frequently, the primary indicator that validates a trend is when it is breached, when the market subsequently makes a sharp move away from the trend line.

In brief, points 1 and 2 in the scenario above only became valid *after* the action at point X had taken place. In the natural progression of a trend there are retracements - price movements that go in the opposite direction to the

---

[15] It is important to note that many traders who do not have a mechanism to validate a trend will simply select arbitrary points.

Trading for a bright future

general trend. Each time these occur, the losing traders gain a little relief from the burden of evidence against their stance. Many of the traders will trade these retracements to bolster their trading stance. But as the trend resumes, they get into trouble and start to place stops at the last top. Other traders who want to gain access to the fruits of the trend will place buy orders to be filled as the market breaks through the last reaction top. Note that the A in the Trend Chart Three is the last reaction top.

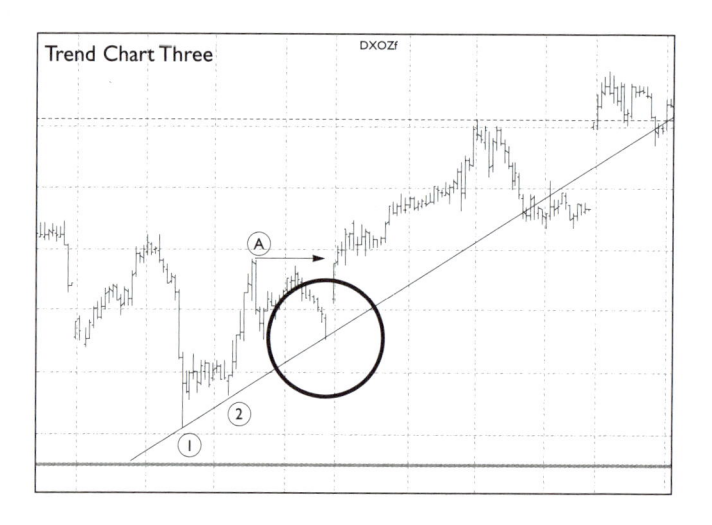

The added 'weight' to the correct trend literally creates a price explosion as the area at the arrow point is pushed through. The mass of orders that follows (bear in mind that a stop placed in the market to protect a trader from going short is also a buy order) creates a further break-away from the trend line. Can you now spot the indicator which gave us the valuable information regarding the validity of points 1 and 2? It is, of course, the action within the larger circle - the breach of the line and then the sharp lift away.

136

Tools and Interpretations

A 'moving average' is an asset's average calculated over a specific period of time. This information is used by traders to identify trends by 'smoothing out' potentially confusing fluctuations in price. For example, a 10 bar moving average includes the last ten bars of an asset's value. The next day, the moving average replaces the latest (which is now the 11th bar) with the most recent bar to calculate the current bar's moving average. Moving averages are often used to obtain the value of an asset over time.

In the search for a true trend, there are some tools that can be of assistance. A wide variety of moving average indicators are available. The best thing for a trader to do when he considers adding one to his strategy is to decide on one and then test it to ensure that it is compatible with what he is trying to achieve. He will need to consider how long a particular moving average may take to cross over. Several types of average can be applied, and the novice trader should take care to familiarise himself with their application.

Managing Market Realities

For the moment, we are going to forget that the market makers have human faces, and concentrate on how they are manifested in the market as actions and movements and on how you can interpret these manifestations and tailor your personal strategy so as to take advantage of them.

Trading for a bright future

Flocking and Herding

In order to trade successfully, you will have to become an observer of both 'herding' and 'flocking' instincts. You must develop the perception to anticipate direction to become enabled to make informed decisions about your trading movements. To make my point easier to follow, I will explain the situation in familiar terms.

Have you ever seen sheepdog trials on television? As a trader, your role will be similar to that of the shepherd, who anticipates the direction of the sheep and then gives commands to his dog. He observes what is happening and issues orders accordingly. The role of the shepherd is *not* to get his dog to chase the sheep, but to employ the dog to use the sheeps' natural progression. When the sheep are travelling in the direction he wants them to go, the dog occupies a non-threatening position in centre or behind.

The shepherd watches the sheeps' heads as they look around for direction indicators and ensure that they are close to the other sheep in the flock. So long as they continue to go in the right direction, the dog is simply instructed to follow. When the shepherd notices that the flock is about to change direction, he instructs the dog to move to prevent it. The sheep see the dog and turn their heads to the other side, which presents no obstacles, and so they take the easy path. At no stage does the shepherd want the flock to cease moving because, should that happen, he would have to bring the dog in more closely. That might cause the sheep either to stand and face the dog, or to run away, creating a difficult to control situation. Herding is supremely tactical, requiring excellent observation skills on the part of the shepherd, who needs

Trading for a bright future

to have complete control over his dog so as to maintain domination of the flock.

During sheep dog trials, there are certain obstacles that the shepherd needs to overcome. There may, for instance, be a short fence with a gap in it, and the sheep have to pass through the gap. As the flock approaches the fence, the animals react to the obstacle with consternation; the gap is narrow and the flock is wide. Their instinct tells them to hold formation and avoid the vulnerability of being in a thinly spread flock. But the shepherd draws them closer and closer until one sheep dashes through the gap, upon which all the rest will follow. As they rush through the fence, the dog runs quickly to the other side in order to maintain control.

When a flock has been over-excited, the animals become nervous and unpredictable. In these circumstances, it is common to see one sheep make a dash for safe ground, and to be followed by the rest of the flock. When the shepherd realises what is happening, he sends his dog in straight away, to frighten the animal and make it join the rest of the flock. He does this *even if the flock was going in the right direction*. Why? Because the moment the shepherd allows the flock to dictate the direction he is at a disadvantage. He *must* retain control at all times. To do so, he consistently applies a limited number of basic principles; he knows the final destination of the flock; he is at a *vantage point*; he is a *critical observer* of flock activity and he has *total control* of the manoeuvring tool.

Let's examine the relationship between the various parties in more detail. Who is in control, and of what? Does the shepherd control the sheep, or the dog? Is the dog in control or merely following instructions? An important

Trading for a bright future

difference between the shepherd and the dog is that the former has a vantage point, offering him a good view of the flock. The dog lacks this advantage, and is only ever able to see one part of the flock at any given time. The shepherd is able, through observing the flock, to anticipate the direction in which it is likely to move. Without the shepherd, the dog really can't function, even though, to the casual observer, oblivious to the instructions of the shepherd, it seems that the dog is in control. This impression is strengthened by the fact that the instructions given may be incomprehensible to anybody but the dog. Let's examine an illustration of the scenario I have just described.

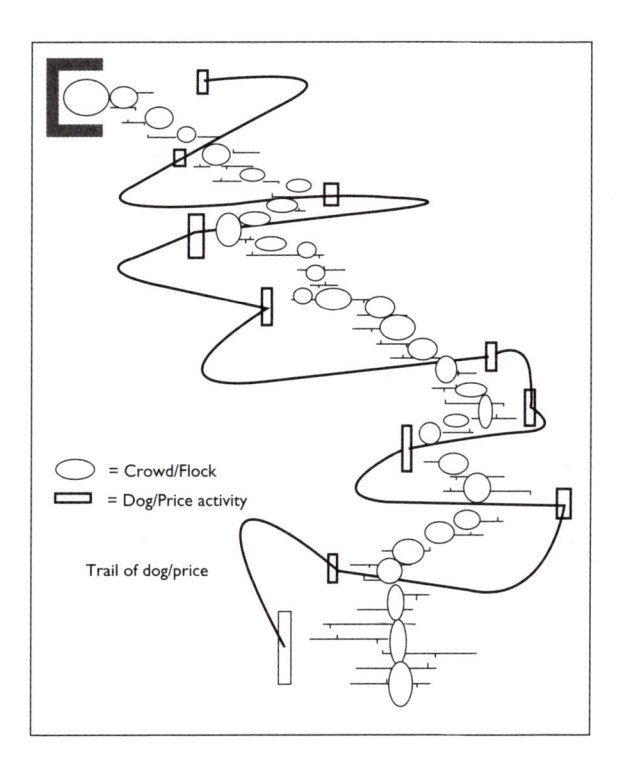

◯ = Crowd/Flock
▭ = Dog/Price activity

Trail of dog/price

The diagram above serves equally well to demonstrate genuine market activity. Overlaid, you can see the 'crowd',

Trading for a bright future

the trail the 'dog' takes and the 'shepherd', overseeing everything.

Now, let's apply the herding metaphor to the world of trading. Read through the preceding passages, exchanging the words 'shepherd' 'dog', 'flock' and 'obstacles' for their equivalents in the trading environment, and you will find that everything I have said continues to apply.

From examining this diagram, it is easy to understand how the overseer (the market maker) can manipulate price activity in order to control and steer the flock. Always bear in mind that the amount of any one stock is invariably limited, so there must be a constant cycle of buying and selling in order to enable the market makers to function in their essential role of working the market - the circularity of the market that we discussed earlier.

The crowd to which I refer is not a physical group of people, but the collective consciousness of the group. This force is what drives the market in any given direction, and that will turn the market at any given point.

Trading for a bright future

A Question of Balance

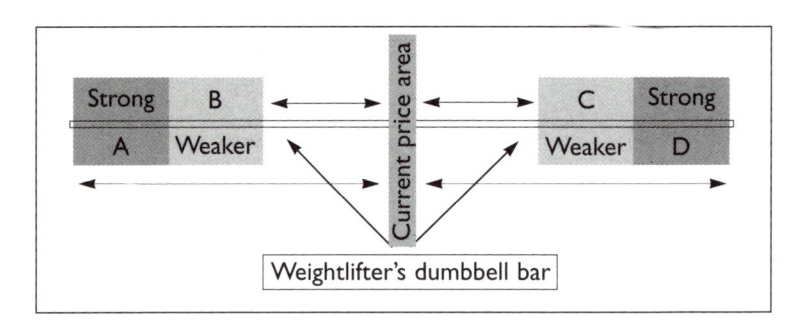

The market, illustrated here in the 'dumb-bell' diagram, is in a constant state of equilibrium. The weights indicated in A, B, C and D, representing opposing sets of beliefs, both strong and weak, are able to slide horizontally along the bar, while areas A and D give the market greater stability. Should either of these strong sets of beliefs start to move towards the centre of the bar, indicating a shift in belief - the market will react accordingly. Areas B and C represent weak, easily questioned beliefs. Doubt can be spread through mere price action among the traders who hold these beliefs, because they do not realise the degree of manipulation to which they are being subjected. Let's examine two separate days with two very different outcomes.

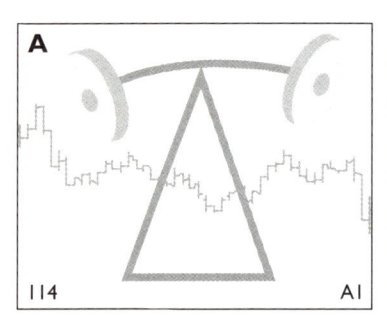

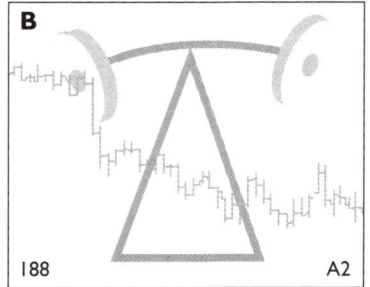

Trading for a bright future

Both charts A1 and A2 illustrate apparently similar movements, but chart A2 experienced a point range of 188, and chart A1 only 114. Such disparities are among the main problems in try to making trading decisions based on chart patterns. They are simply too subjective.

Chart A2 is an excellent illustration of how a change in belief structures can affect a market, because of the apparently 'flat' area that can be seen before the sharp fall away to new lows.

In the A1 chart, the weaker areas - illustrated by B and C in the previous diagram 'weightlifter' image - were moving the market. Although the market travelled some 114 points between the extreme high and the extreme low, there was considerable up and down movement within the 114 points.

On the A2 chart, you can see that the market remained balanced for a period, and then tipped sharply, covering the overall fall of 188 points.

In the A1 example, the market was being moved by the areas B and C from the earlier 'weightlifter' image - those representing the weak holders. There was no real commitment to any overall direction until the end of the period when new lows were reached.

The A2 chart shows a very different sequence of events, one of the equilibrium at the beginning of the day, and then a definite commitment to the low side of the market. To use the weightlifting equipment to demonstrate, this would be the equivalent to the 'sliding' of one set of the strong and the weaker weights towards the other end of the weight lifter's bar - in layman's terms, a large percentage of traders had a change of opinion with regard to the value of the stock.

Movement of the market revolves around the ever fluctuating collective consciousness of beliefs. The art of successful trading involves understanding that the markets are *not random*, but well-organised and controlled, understanding the current predominant belief structure, being in a position to know the condition of the current belief structure, the ability to understand when belief structures are being manipulated, and the ability to recognise a fundamental shift in belief structures.

The trader should always remember that the market makers are in a very privileged position - they have immense power and can even influence governmental decisions at some levels

At their disposal is the knowledge of how much stock is floating and how much is fixed and the knowledge of institutional money. They can assess strength and weakness in any given stock at any given moment in time, and they have the best information technology in the world to deliver all this information at a moment's notice.

•

A thorough and clearheaded understanding of the realities of market activity is essential to successful trading. Maintaining an efficient, unemotional decision structure is just as important, and this is the point to which we now turn.

CHAPTER ELEVEN

The Psychology of Decision Making

In trading, decision making must never be made in the heat of the moment. Decisions *must always* be part of your overall strategy. The market will certainly not stay on hold just because you don't know what to do. You will develop and maintain a balance between forward planning and flexibility in your trading, and acquire the ability to monitor and maintain your decision making process.

Before you plunge into the world of trading, you will need to learn how to practise forming a behavioural sequence that will lead you through even the most fraught situation towards a calm, unemotional decision.

By now, you have inspected your personal circumstances, and are aware of the strengths and weaknesses that lie within them. Having passed through this vital stage on the path towards successful trading, you are now ready to move on. Let's examine the decision making processes of both the successful and the unsuccessful trader.

Decision Structure of Successful Trader

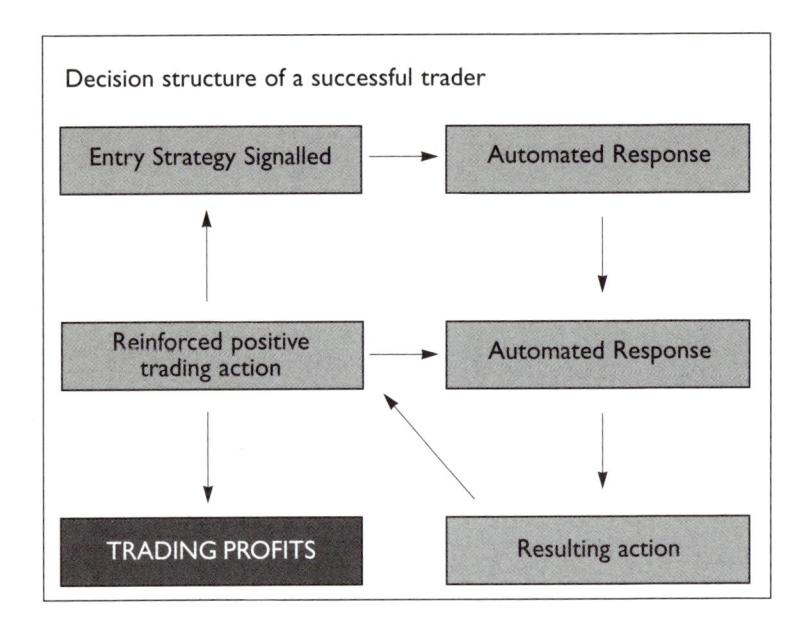

```
Decision structure of a successful trader

    Entry Strategy Signalled  ──►  Automated Response
              ▲                              │
              │                              ▼
    Reinforced positive       ──►  Automated Response
     trading action
              │                              │
              ▼                              ▼
      TRADING PROFITS                 Resulting action
```

Consider the implications of the diagram above. Because, in a real-life trading situation, nobody can win all the time, it is always possible that the trader's action might result in a losing trade. Nonetheless, this may still be considered to be a positive trading action. How? In fact, the ability to recognise the inclusion of occasional losses into a generally successful trading pattern is one of the principal differences between the amateur and the professional. The successful trader has already defined and validated his or her strategy, *knows* that it produces profits over time, that one must wait and implement the predetermined plan, and accepts that, once in a while, there will be a loss. The ability to accept occasional loss is part of a trader's strength. He never takes a trading failure as a personal affront.

Trading for a bright future

Decision Structure of an Unsuccessful Trader

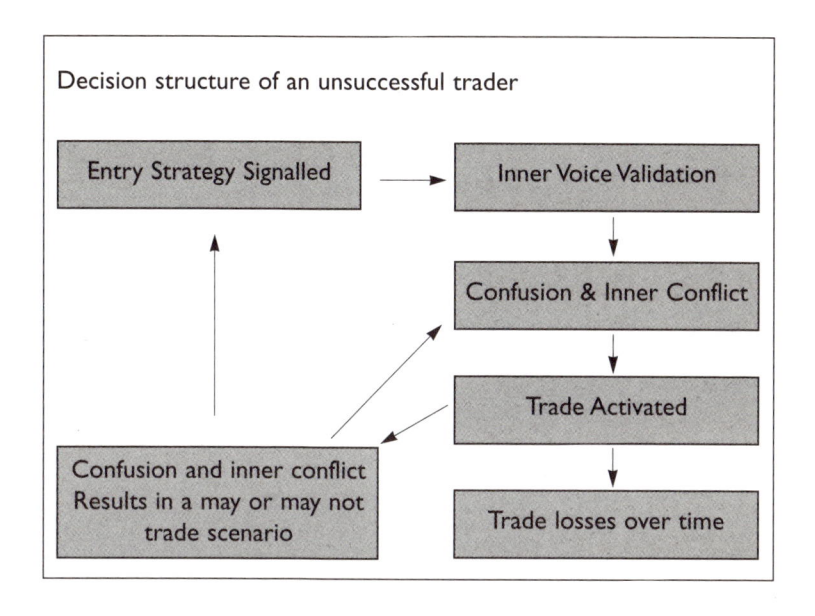

```
Decision structure of an unsuccessful trader

  Entry Strategy Signalled  ──►  Inner Voice Validation
           ▲                              │
           │                              ▼
           │                   Confusion & Inner Conflict
           │          ┌──────────────►    │
           │          │                   ▼
  Confusion and inner conflict       Trade Activated
  Results in a may or may not             │
       trade scenario                     ▼
                                   Trade losses over time
```

An amateur does not have a workable action plan, and consequently lacks a consistent response. He does not have a clear idea of what does or does not work, and is inclined towards random behaviour. If a trade is activated according to the scheme outlined above, each of the conditions will become part of the trader's routine behaviour, and every time a strategy is signalled, the same process will swing into action. The trader will lose for as long as this unworkable loop is maintained, and will also become prone to the associated problems of conflict, anger and sickness. It is not unusual for a trader to continue in this situation for a number of years, until the inevitable outcomes of bankruptcy, blaming the market, and renouncing trading. Sadly, it is not uncommon for this fraught situation to lead to problems in the trader's personal life, as he lashes out in frustration at those around him. Fortunately, an awareness of the potential problems, and a willingness to devote time to planning, developing and testing a strategy means than it is possible to avoid becoming caught in a destructive loop such as the one outlined above.

The Circularity of Strategy

Trading is not difficult. It is simply a matter of acquiring a strategy and sticking to it. Strategy, like the movement of stock within the market, is circular. If your risk reward ratio is working within your strategy then all you have to do is initiate a circle that starts with placing a trade and ends with taking either a loss or a profit.

The definition of madness is said to be doing the same thing and expecting to get different results. Many traders are doing the same thing every day and expecting things to get better! These traders will not get improve their performances until they start to initiate circles that have predefined closing points and work within a defined strategy.

Managing your decisions
The Two Essential Steps Towards Activating a Trade

The first thing that you should do before activating a trade is to learn how to identify a signal - an indication, based on the formulae, data and charts that you use in market analysis, that it is time to buy or sell a particular investment - or that a market trend is shifting - and to accept it. The second is to cultivate the response to that signal.

Trading for a bright future

This is *learned behaviour*, and the process is relatively straightforward.

Let's examine the process of learning in an ordinary environment. Humans, like all living beings, respond to the environment they are in, and to the events which occur around them. There is usually a reaction to their response, and with time, the event or environment becomes familiar. A template for future responses in similar circumstances has been created, enabling the subject to predict the outcome, and even influence it to some extent.

The trader has to adjust this basic learning process to the market because, in this environment, while events may be similar, no two will ever be exactly the same. Trading strategies must be able to deal with this lack of consistency. This is an important hurdle to overcome at the beginning of a trading career. Furthermore, once one has committed to making a trade, there is generally *no way* to influence the outcome. As the trader is invariably in a situation that is entirely new, there are little grounds with which to predict it. To the unprepared, this situation can be confusing and frustrating, and one can feel as lost as in a gambling environment.

While the unprepared trader flounders in uncharted waters, his professional colleague is confident in employing the systematic, tested formula that he *knows* will deliver trading profits. His decisions occur within the boundaries of a *flexible but pre-planned formula*. By employing foresight the professional has stacked the odds in his favour. The plan is in action, rendering neutral the problems of unknown variables, the inability to influence the outcome of the situation and the emotional potency of the current trade. From a detached stance, the professional is poised, observant and controlled. Not for him the hot-headedness that hinders the execution of further strategies involving the increase of contract size or exiting from the position. By behaving in a manner consistent with the strategy that he has already designed, his emotions have simply been removed from the equation.

You and the Market

The way you view the markets is of immense importance to your success as a trader. Every time you win, somebody else loses. How does that affect the way you feel? You don't care? Of course, you don't know the loser so that person may be of no consequence to you. On the other hand, no-one is without a conscience. While feeling of having gained at another's expense rarely prevent one from trading, they can curb one's ambitions, placing a limit on the desired degree of success and inhibiting attempts to gain really large profits.

This description may not seem to apply to you, but are you really sure? Question yourself carefully and ask what exactly it is that you wish to take from the market. This is an issue that few traders really look into, but that does not mean that it is not important. Your answer, after honest reflection, may indicate future success or failure.

Let the Market be your Guide

Golfers have told me that the worst thing that an aspiring player can do is to pick up a club and take an uncoached swing. The novice instinctively assumes the posture that is most comfortable - generally not the one that is most suited for playing golf. Similarly, the worst thing you can do is enter the market unprepared. If you adopt an untutored stance, you will not be trading for long, and you will leave the market with empty pockets.

People often learn from watching others and copying them. This technique is of limited use in a market environment, as no two actions are ever the same and the trader may not be fully aware of the implications of the situation he observes. Rather than trying to learn an immovable reaction to a specific set of circumstances, you should learn how to react flexibly to whichever situation the market throws up at you. A trader cannot learn from copying another person, the only way to move forward is to develop one's own technique.

The ability to recognise the importance of thoughtful personal advancement is one of the prime differences between the professional and the amateur trader. Typically, an amateur buys a few books about trading, gets a charting package and draws up a few trend lines. Innocently, the novice enters the market and is shocked to discover that, far from being a gold mine, it can be a harsh adversary. The way in which the budding trader reacts to this reality shock can determine whether success or failure lies ahead.

The Emotions of Failure

In ordinary circumstances, fear is a healthy emotion, serving to warn us of, and protect us from, danger. But our interpretations of what represents a potential danger are not always correct. Ignorance or an incomplete understanding of something often causes it to be much more frightening that it needs to be, much as children fear what they do not understand, and imagine things lurking in shadows that cannot really be there.

Rather than fleeing from something that alarms or upsets us, we should try to look at the situation objectively and understand exactly what it is all about. Frequently, the understanding banishes fear.

The new trader usually experiences feelings best described as a mixture of fear and excitement. When things go well, the trader feels excited, and if badly, nervous or afraid. It can be extremely difficult to tell the difference between the two emotions. The more intense the feelings caused by trading are, and the more difficult it becomes to distinguish between fear and excitement, the more critical you will become of trading opportunities. If this situation continues unchecked, severe trading problems will drastically hinder your performance.

The good news is that trading fear tends to build up gradually, so there is plenty of time to check it before it causes damage and weakens your performance!

A confidence crisis generally develops in three stages. The trader's insecurity regarding trading protocol causes a dip in confidence levels. Then, a false sense of confidence can develop, as the trader begins to feel comfortable in a trading environment, and familiar with the protocol. Then again, as losses remain unaccounted for in the absence of a strategy, the groundless confidence disappears, and the trader is left performing ineffectively.

A fear of the unknown emerges as the trader begins to experience the negative emotions that I have described, and this fear is exacerbated by uncertainties of price, volume, current activities, impending announcements, and so on. Together, these elements form an unknown entity, which looms anonymously behind the trader, exerting a vast amount of control and energy over him.

Working Towards Consistent Success

A successful trader has become caught in a success loop, even though, like the unsuccessful trader, he is only partly aware of his situation. Many successful traders are acting on a level so instinctive that they are unable to explain exactly what it is that they are doing. Trying to unravel their trading behaviour might even have a detrimental effect on their performance. Some successful traders have written books about their success, and others on reading them, have tried to emulate them. These attempts are often disastrous, because the writer has not been able to communicate the whole story. If the trader has been successful for many years, his success loop will be deeply rooted in his subconscious, and he may be operating on an entirely intuitive level. He may not even really understand what he is doing, but simply enjoys supreme confidence in his abilities and his growing trading account.

For you to find yourself in this privileged position you must learn how to define what a success loop is, learn the methods by which you can enter the success loop, build a strategy that suits you and develop the tools necessary to maintain your success.

You, as a successful trader, must have a well-defined trading strategy, complete faith in your strategy, an automatic response mechanism, a long-term outlook, confidence in your abilities, a strong sense of purpose, and a developed sense of feeling the market. The unsuccessful trader may have a well-defined strategy without the other components necessary for success, or a poor trading strategy, incomplete faith in his strategy, a cherry-picking response mechanism, a short term win mentality, a low level of confidence, a casual attitude, and a poor or non-existent ability to feel the market.

The trader that consistently loses has developed a losing strategy. Over time, he has become psychologically attached to this approach, which is maintained in the hope of winning the next big trade. The trader can become so deeply attached to his strategy, that he will, as strange as it seems, defend it in the face of all the evidence against it. His behaviour is very like that of a person trapped in an unhappy relationship who struggles on, even though to all around it is clear that he is in a losing situation.

This attachment is *emotional*, not *logical*. The trader has become stuck in a destructive loop, which has created its own strategy, and which has become - as in the case of the successful trader - so instinctive to his performance that it is operating at a subconscious level. It is very difficult to break out of the loop, but if this is not achieved the trader's account will be emptied. There are even cases where the trader has a subconscious wish to stop trading completely, and his destructive behaviour is his psyche's way of granting it to him.

●

The emerging trader's real challenge is to be consciously aware of everything that is behind the trade *at the moment* of making it. This awareness is what distinguishes the successful from the unsuccessful. The successful trader has performed, with no emotional overlay, in accordance with his strategy. His mind is clear and prepared to process the continuous stream of market data that is arriving. The successful trader's challenge is to maintain this state of functioning in a non-emotive environment.

A paper trader is often capable of achieving excellent results over prolonged periods, but as soon as he enters the market for real, everything changes. So, to become successful traders, we need to learn how to be 'paper traders' in live circumstances - just as calm and composed as if real money was not at stake.

Trading for a bright future

CHAPTER TWELVE

'The Curse of the Lollipop'

Few, if any, guides to trading discuss the power that the subconscious has over trading behaviour. My experience has taught me that it is far too significant to overlook. The insight that my training and work in hypnotherapy gave me have provided me with the means to 'lift the lid' on some of the inner workings of the brain, and to examine how they affect training.

In the normal day to day environment, any task - from picking up a coffee cup to negotiating a flight of stairs - is conducted using past experience as a model. All of our experiences are recorded in our subconscious minds, available for instant retrieval *without* conscious awareness. The subconscious is a complex mechanism, and associations between events are often much less straightforward than one might expect.

The title of this chapter refers to a case I dealt with some years ago - when I was working as a hypnotherapist - which illustrates the type of emotional association that can be so problematic in trading. I was consulted by a woman who suffered from an excessive hand washing affliction. This had begun following a small car accident that had left her rather upset. Over the years that followed the accident, her condition had worsened to the point where her hands actually bled from the washing. Her life and family were deeply affected by her problem, but despite all her efforts to rationalise and deal with what was happening, she could not break the cycle and stop the obsessive washing.

Working together, my client and I finally arrived at the incident in her childhood that had resulted in the birth of the problem. Under hypnosis, she recalled the important occasion. She was standing beside her mother at the kitchen sink enjoying a cherry lollipop when she was told to tie her shoe-lace. The little girl reached up, placed the lollipop on the work surface and bent down to tie her lace. As she did, the sweet rolled onto the floor, whereupon she picked it up and put it in her mouth. Suddenly angry, the mother shouted and slapped the little girl, shaking her violently as she explained with great drama all the terrible things that germs could do to her.

An *emotional event* of huge proportions had occurred, and it was locked away in the child's subconscious only to emerge years later at the prompting of the stress caused by the car accident. As her mind struggled to deal with the accident, it latched on to the childhood incident, prompted by the similar emotions that the two quite different events brought about.

Never underestimate the power of the subconscious mind and the way in which it protects and nurtures you throughout your life. The incident described above, might not seem to an adult to be significant enough to result in the condition suffered by my client, but when it occurred, the subconscious had to handle it as best it could for the child's protection. In such situations, the subconscious often locks the memory and the *emotional content* of the experience away where they cannot readily be accessed. The concept of 'locking away' is important to your understanding of the following examples and discussion.

Day to Day Life and the Subconscious

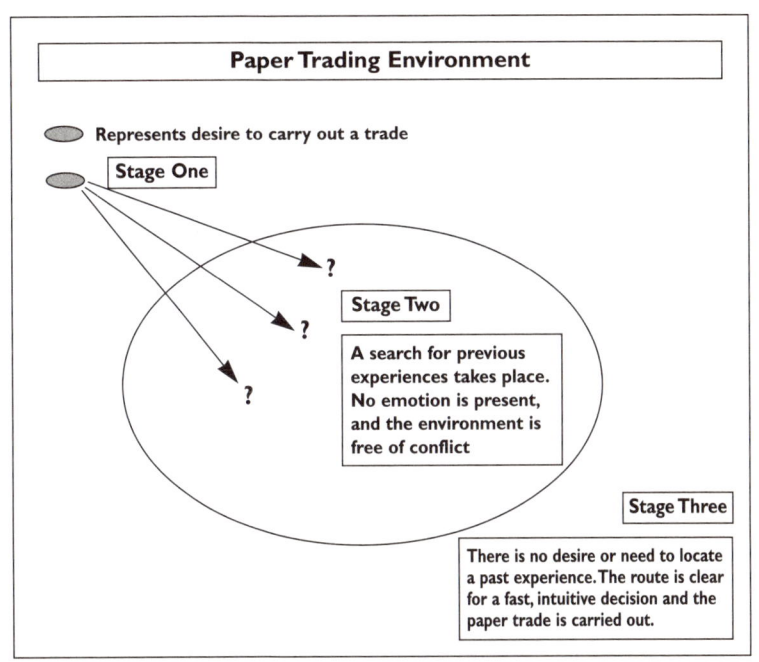

Paper Trading Environment

Represents desire to carry out a trade

Stage One

Stage Two
A search for previous experiences takes place. No emotion is present, and the environment is free of conflict

Stage Three
There is no desire or need to locate a past experience. The route is clear for a fast, intuitive decision and the paper trade is carried out.

In the normal day to day task environment illustrated above, we are able to operate very efficiently - we do not have to think about how to pick up a coffee cup, how to bring it to our lips, how to prevent it spilling and how to put it down before we are able to take a drink. We simply carry out the task with an 'autopilot' response. These responses are like well worn paths - it is very hard to deviate from them. Try using the opposite hand to the one you usually do and you'll see that your actions are not nearly so smooth and automatic.

Trading for a bright future

Now, beginning with an examination of the paper trading environment, we'll move towards the act of trading and examine the vast differences between this environment and the everyday one.

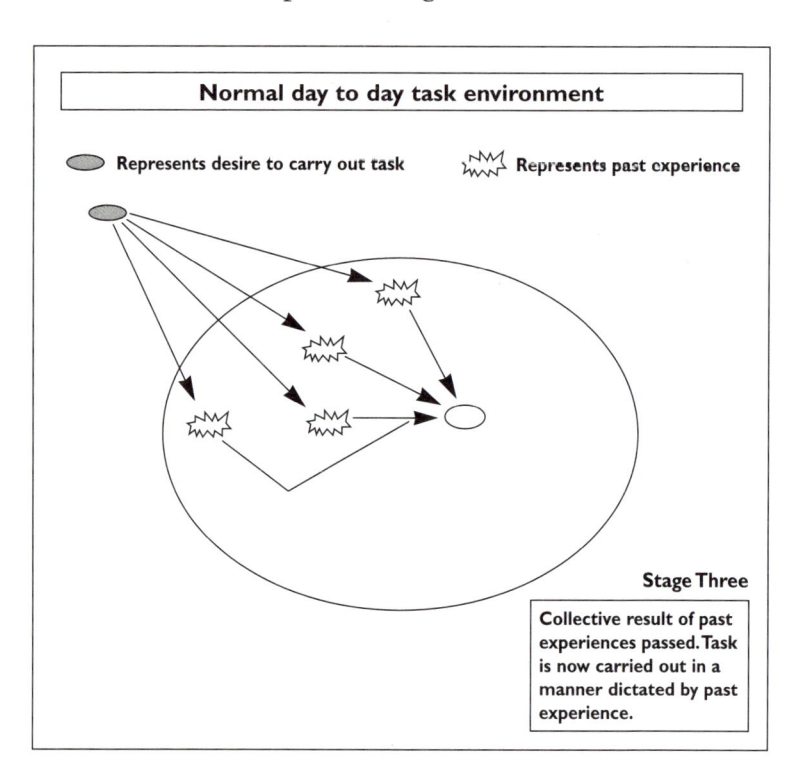

The Paper Trading Environment

Normal day to day task environment

⬤ Represents desire to carry out task   〰️ Represents past experience

Stage Three

Collective result of past experiences passed. Task is now carried out in a manner dictated by past experience.

In the diagram above, stage one represents the desire to carry out a trade, in the context of a paper trading environment. In stage two, the mind scans - rather like a radar screen - for a previous experience with the components it seeks. As there is no real emotion in the paper trading environment, the mind finds little, if anything, to question in carrying out the trade, resulting in a fast, intuitive action.

160

Trading for a bright future

As more and more paper trades are carried out, the response to paper trading gets more and more intuitive and uncomplicated. Traders in this environment are often able to produce outstanding results that convince them that the time is right to do it for real!

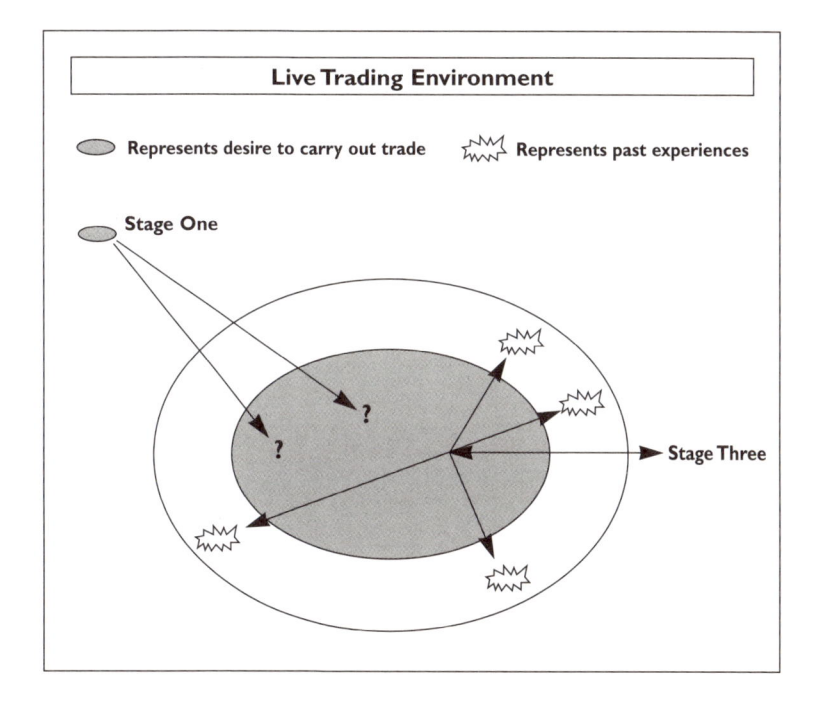

The Live Trading Environment

In the live trading environment, illustrated above, the desire to carry out the trade is clearly present and, as in the case of paper trading, the trader's mind begins to scan through all of his memories, searching for a comparable experience against which to judge his current situation.

Now however, emotion is present, completely altering the trader's mental environment. Because no two events are ever the same in trading, he will not find a suitable event to serve as a model for his behaviour. In fact, the mind only has *emotional content* on which to form the basis of a search. In other words, it will automatically begin to scan for memories associated with similar emotions to those felt at the time of trading.

If, because he is trading live, the trader's current emotion is fear, the subconscious mind will locate *memories associated with fear*. Invariably, the memory of a fearful event is located, resulting in a strong association between trading and fear. The next time the trader picks up the phone, the mind has automatically mapped a pathway to fear. This is reinforced every time he trades until he simply cannot trade without being afraid.

Decisions taken in a fearful state of mind do not produce good results. Most frequently, they cause traders to enter the market in completely the wrong direction, causing a loss and thus releasing the trader from a fearful situation. The subconscious, in short, does all it can to prevent the trader from experiencing negative emotions, to the extent of pushing him towards failure and removing him from the stressful environment.

Trading for a bright future

The Birth of the Lollipop

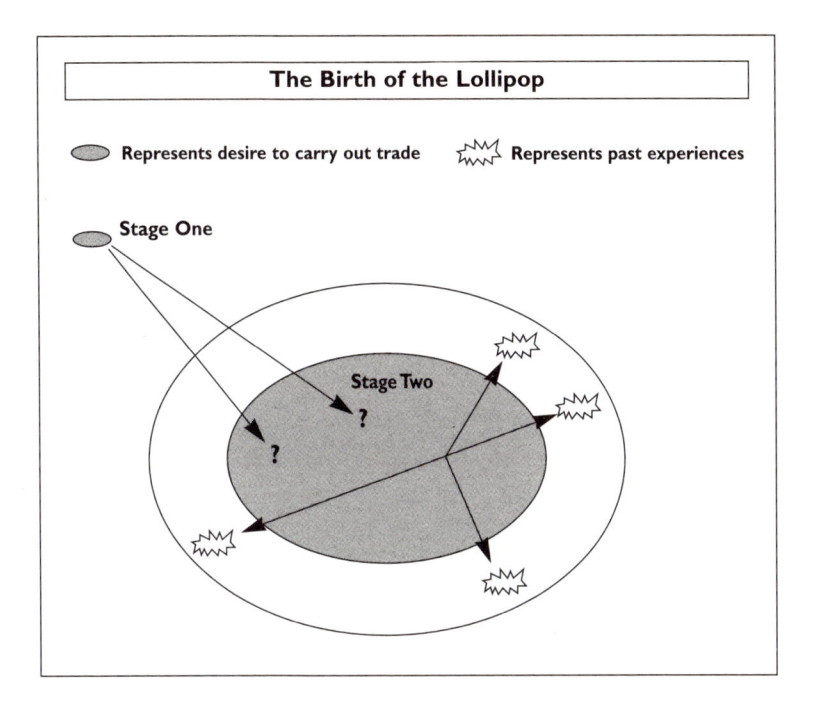

```
                    The Birth of the Lollipop

    ⬭  Represents desire to carry out trade     ⚡  Represents past experiences

    ⬭ Stage One

                        Stage Two
                           ?
                      ?
```

Over a period of time, psychological paths to negative emotions may become deeper and deeper. The trader who finds himself in this position becomes totally irrational in his trading behaviour - a situation that often results in an endless search for a means to escape inner conflict and turmoil, from the latest software fad to esoteric trading guidance.

Professional help may be the only answer for the trader who finds himself in this situation. Inner reflection and a period away from the market are certainly very important.

Trading for a bright future

•

Successful traders need to locate a trading method or technique that allows them to take their decisions unemotionally, bypassing the subconscious association between trading and fear. A strategy is always the same, and if the trader adheres to it, is operated in an emotion-free way, which does not admit the problematic elements of fear, subconscious association and unnecessary failures.

Recognising the power inherent in the subconscious is the most important step to take in neutralising its potential to damage your trading success.

CHAPTER THIRTEEN

The Wrap-up

Traders become bankrupt for a variety of reasons, including risking too much money, lacking an exit strategy, a dearth of numeracy and the failure to understand risk. All of these problems can be avoided with careful preparation and diligence.

Manage your money. Always ask yourself 'how much?' and 'how many?'. Using stop losses does not represent money management! If you are going to trade multiple contracts, you will need a mechanism that is part of your proven strategy to increase in size. Part of this strategy should be letting the market tell you how many to buy or sell, and when.

To keep money under control, you should keep trades as small as possible for as long as possible, never average down, but always up, avoid becoming obsessed with doubling your money, withdraw money from the market at regular intervals.

Keeping trades as small as possible for as long as possible simply means that there is time for you to become a professional trader, one who does not focus on money, but on interpreting the market correctly and consistently. When this is carried out, profits will follow. When you find yourself in a losing position, never buy or sell again in the same direction to average your cost down - this could be a disastrous move.

Trends persist and should be followed until you are stopped out by a reversal, or until your exit strategy comes into force. Trading for profit will cause you to focus on the money - a negative strategy, as there will always be some degree of desire to take money from the market. You will close profitable trades long before trends end, reducing your win-to-lose ratio.

Although most traders focus on points of entry to the market, most lose money. Unless you are doing some very short term style of trading, entry position is the least important aspect of trading - your exit strategy is much more crucial if you hope to trade successfully over the long term.

Dealing with losses is a matter of adjusting your attitude. Losing traders believe that losses are a reflection on their own personality, and lose self-esteem every time they lose money. They believe that loss is liable to continue, coupled with the idea that they must never lose while trading. Winning traders accept that losses are part of the business, and do not assume that a loss is a reflection of their personalities. A certain amount of loss in trading is inevitable, and this has to be accepted. Winning traders focus on the fact that money is not important - trading skills are. Learn to develop them in a flawless fashion, and develop the quality trade mentality. Learn to ask yourself whether your trade was consistent with the rules of your strategy, whether you are happy with the way it was carried out, and whether you could carry out another trade in the same manner. The ability to answer 'yes' to this questions demonstrates that you are building a quality trade mentality, that you are focussing on the *overall concept of trading* and not on individual trades.

While losing traders believe that the entire market is rigged, that only insiders make money and that the market is random, winning traders know that while the market is controlled and manipulated to some degree, they can join the professionals in making a profit through applying their knowledge and skills.

Losing traders have a variety of motivating factors. Some believe that trading is a hobby or a casual affair, some that it is an uphill push every day, some that it is easy and anybody should be able to do it. Winning traders know that it is a stimulating and exciting challenge and they know that only a minority of traders will reach the skill level necessary for persistent success.

Losing traders believe that the 'inside' professionals or market makers always win, and cost them money, and that the market gains at their expense. They want revenge for what the market has done to them. Winning traders know that they are ultimately responsible for every resulting action that does or does not take place in the market environment; that they alone are the direct cause of every trading profit or loss. They determine how much of a trading profit or loss they are prepared to accept.

Losing traders believe that the market has a direct, aggressive personality. Winning traders know that the market has no personality at all, other than that which they project onto it. They know that if they start to think or communicate to others about the market in emotive terms, they have made a fundamental shift in their trading, one that moves them away from the automatic proven strategy mode to that of autonomic functioning (the fight or flight response).

Losing traders always demonstrate a casual overall attitude, and are frequently lazy and sloppy. Winning traders know that trading is not easy, that it is a skill that has to be learned and honed to perfection over time. Most have experienced failure, and have learned from the experience.

Losing traders believe that by reading papers and listening to brokers, research news and trading magazines; they have all the information they need. Winning traders believe that their proven strategy provides them with all the tools they need to get the job done. Strategy development takes time and effort and is often a laborious process, but the lack of a strategy results in trading losses and ultimately, the need to leave the trading environment.

GLOSSARY

Accumulation: Buying that occurs over a period of time avoiding a single, substantial purchase that could drive up the market price. More specifically, buying which leads to the gradual build-up (to accumulate) a position. Accumulation is generally characterised by the absorption of excess supply in the market, generally practised when a stock, commodity or the market in general has a long, low sideways period. The accumulator absorbs any selling by nibbling - constantly buying up and accumulating a position, being careful not to buy too much as to raise the price until the sellers (supply or weak holders) are mostly sold out of the market.

Actions: The price movement and volume of the overall market or stock.

Ask price: The price at which a security is offered for purchase. Also known as the offer price.

Asset: An item of value owned by an individual or corporation, particularly one that can be converted to cash.

Bar chart: A bar chart is a chart that represents market

Trading for a bright future

activity with a 'high' and a 'low'. It represents the price movement within a time period as a vertical bar, often with horizontal branches representing the open and close prices. This is the type of chart most commonly used by traders for studying trends in the market.

Below the market: Taking the market to be the current price, below the current price.

Bid price: Price which a player in the market/a party to the transaction is prepared to pay for a given security.

BF line: The anticipated average price paid, of all transactions that day.

Bond: Essentially, a type of IOU issued for a time frame of more than one year with the purpose of raising intention of raising capital by borrowing. Governments, cities, corporations and other institutions sell bonds. The person that buys a bond is paid interest on the sum originally invested.

Broker: A broker is someone who deals in a commodity.

Bull phase: Period during which it is generally believed that the market, or a section of it, is about to rise in price or is rising.

Bundling: This term refers to the practice of combining similar products and selling them together.

Cash market: That in which actual commodities or

Trading for a bright future

equities are bought and sold for immediate settlement.

Charting package: Software that enables you to graph trends or other visual representations in a market

Cherry picking: The best way to understand this term is to imagine that you are actually picking cherries; the one just out of reach is always sweeter. The trader thinks, 'I won't take this trade, I'll wait for a better one'.

Collective consciousness: In market terms, the sum total of thoughts, feelings, hopes, desires, wish fulfilment and any other thought element, is within the active and non active (those waiting to trade) trading body that we call 'the crowd'.

Contract: The unit of trade for a financial or commodity future.

Contract expiry: Futures are traded on a three-month basis, and when the contract comes to the end of its term it is said to *expire*. You still trade in the next contract before the expiry of the most recent one. Some traders will trade across different contract periods as a form of minimising risk.

Datafeed: Generally referred to as a stream of data from a combination of exchanges that combines these different streams of data usually into a single composite stream and allows you to feed this data, typically, into your PC. Users generally receive this information via satellite, straight line or, increasingly, the Internet.

Derivatives: A derivative is generally a financial instrument whose characteristics and value are dependent on those of an underlying instrument or asset.

Disavowal: The trader in disavowal refuses to acknowledge something, as for example, as in the case of the person who refuses to even broach the subject of the possibility of there being a fundamental flaw in the strategy that is being used.

Downside: the potential loss involved in an investment or activity.

Dow Jones Averages: This refers to the world famous averages of market values (generally American) complied by Dow Jones and Company. The other two that are generally consulted are the Dow Jones Transportation Average and the Dow Jones Utility Average.

Dow Jones Composite Average: a market indicator that averages 65 stocks in 3 different categories to determine how the main US market as a whole is progressing.

Dow Jones Industrial Average: The world's best known index of stocks, often simply referred to as 'the Dow'. This is an equally weighted composite calculation of the top 30 Industrial sector stocks in the United States. As industries wax and wane, stocks are either added or deleted from the group.

Drawdown: Although the technically minded might not agree with me, I see this as another way of saying that you have lost money. Your trading strategy is currently resulting in losses, and money is being withdrawn from your account. A drawdown is typically referred to by system traders in referring to a losing period on an account. People assessing systems will usually be very interested in the 'maximum drawdown' of the account over a period of time. This refers to the maximum loss situation in the account balance over a period of time.

Emotive overlay: An emotional or non-rational action or reaction to internal or external influences that affects your ability to trade.

Entry strategy: A strategy for entering the market.

Exercise: The implementation of the rights of an option, by buying or selling the underlying asset.

Exhaustion trading: This occurs when the market has set up on a BF day, and the trader is expecting a substantial move. However, instead of opening close to the mid line of the set up day and then climbing or falling a long way enabling the trader to trade with the prevailing trend, it opens at a price that is a hundred or more points above or below the BF mid line, exhausting the potential trading range. The market may then be traded on the basis that it has exhausted the directional move and will now tend to drift back towards the mid line price.

Expiration date: The date on which an option expires, and becomes valueless if it is not exercised (by buying or selling the underlying asset). This may also refer to the last traded day on a futures contract.

Expire: To come to an end.

Fear and excitement: In effect, these emotions are often one and the same, characterised by symptoms that include a racing heart, sweating, deep breathing and heightened awareness.

Feedback loop: When a trade has been initiated in the right manner it develops positive feedback.

Fixed stock: An unchanging financial instrument, signifying an ownership position in a corporation, representing a proportionate claim on a share of the corporations assets.

Floating stock: Stock which is available for trading by the public. Sometimes referred to as 'the float', or supply.

Flocking: In trading, the tendency of the majority of outside traders to go for 'safety in numbers' - effectively turning them into an emotional, easily manipulated group, at the mercy of the market makers.

Flotation: Making stock available for sale to the public to allow the original owners and early investors to access the profits they have made.

Futures: A future is a contract that requires delivery of a bond, commodity, etc. at a specific price, and on a specific date. May also be referred to as a 'futures contract'. In the case of Index Futures (futures that trade as a derivative of the underlying stock index), the delivery simply involves the settlement of the difference between the underlying instrument and the expiring future on a chosen date at a specific time of day.

Gambling environment: Because we have all heard the stories of amateur traders' losses, trading in general in often compared to gambling. It is the amateur's inconsistency and haphazardness that creates this environment, not trading of itself.

Gap closure theory: Based around the concept that gaps in a chart must have price activity through them. Not a theory held by everybody.

Gap up, gap down: A sudden leap or fall in price with no traded prices in between. Most common on the open of a market from the previous night's close price.

Gapped market: The end of the trading day gives us a closing price. At the open of the market on the following morning there will be an open price. If this open price is above the close price then the market has gapped up. Similarly, if the market opens below the close the market has gapped down.

Getting filled: The fulfilment of your order in the market.

Going long: Entering a market with the anticipation of higher prices (bullish). Buying into a market.

Going short: entering a market with the anticipation of

lower prices (bearish). Selling into a market.

In the money: When a trade has been initiated and the price is above the designated buy or when a sale has occurred and the price is currently below the sale price. Also referred to in options trading, when an option is above its strike price in the case of having bought a call or below the strike price in the place of a put.

Inner voice: The still, small voice inside each of us, it can be a positive attribute or a negative one.

Institutional investors: Entities with a large amount to invest, such as a company or bank or more commonly a fund.

Intuitive trading: Best defined as a sense of knowing, understanding and a deep psychological awareness of the condition of the market, and what is going to constitute a profitable trade.

Jobber: The person who acts as primary actor in the buying and selling of financial securities.

Limit order: Order to a broker to buy a specified quantity of a security at or below a specified price, or to sell it at or above a specified price relative the current market price.

Local stop: Stop in the vicinity of where you initiated your trade, thereby restricting loss.

Loop: A behavioural pattern. In trading, learned reflexes

Trading for a bright future

to trading circumstances.

Lot: A number of shares, often 100, sold collectively.

Market (stock): The organised trading of stocks through exchanges - any organisation or group that maintains a market place for the purchase and sale of options, securities, etc..

Market makers: A brokerage or bank that maintains an ask and bid price in a particular security, by remaining in a position to buy or sell at a fixed price, known as 'making a market'.

Market order: A buy or sell order in which the broker is to execute the order at the best price currently available. Often stockbrokers have made arrangements with market makers and you will not get the best price available, so it is wise to use limit orders, allowing you to force the broker or market maker to execute and fulfil your order at the limit price or better rather than at the price he wants to fill it at.

Movements: Change in value, rate, or price.

Moving a stop: Moving your stop to maximise profit or minimise potential loss.

Moving average (simple): The average price of a security over a certain period of time (for example, twenty bars).

Moving average cross-over: The point where a shorter

moving average (drawn over less bars) moves over the longer moving average, indicating a possible change of trend direction.

Offer price: See **Ask price.**

Options: The right to buy (call option) or sell (put option) a certain type equity, future, commodity or other security, for a certain price at a particular time.

Outsider: A normal trader, who is not privy to information that the market makers have, including, of course, the unsuspecting general public.

Paper trader: A person who makes simulated transactions, with no real exchange of money, to test and practice theories.

Pit traders: The 'pit' refers to an area on the trading floor where the traders who still buy and sell in person conduct business.

Point range: Range of points, from highest to lowest, on a trading chart.

Portfolio: Collection of investments owned by the same person or institution.

Pre-defined strategy: A trading methodology/ system that has been defined and evaluated in advance.

Professional money: Large corporations with interests in the market and the market makers.

Pyramiding: This is the technique of using profits earned on open positions to purchase additional securities. It is a learned skill, which distinguishes the professional trader from the novice. It should never be carried out just because you have a feeling that a trade is good and is going to go a long way. All increases in size should fall within your proven strategy, of which pyramiding becomes a stand-alone component which may or may not be activated in any given trade, in the manner of a computer program that lays dormant until called into action.

Rally: A substantial rise in price of a commodity, stock, or the market in general, following a dip or pause in price action.

Reaction: A drop in the price of a stock, bond, commodity, index, or the overall market, following a rise or vice versa.

Rejection tick: A steady increase in ticks, followed by a rapidly marked up price, and immediate marking down, illustrated as an isolated point on a tick chart or vice versa.

Retracements: A price reaction that 'retraces', i.e. goes back over the recent price action, usually measured as a percentage of the total move.

Risk-reward ratio: The ratio of the amount you are prepared to risk relative to the profit target.

Roll-over: The transition between an expiring future and the one taking over as the active contract. In terms of financial futures, this often takes place on the third Thursday or Friday of the month preceding expiry month. Financial futures generally trade using the months March, June, September and December.

Security: A legal document, usually issued by a large corporation, that proves debt.

Sell-off: A sudden, radical drop in price as a result of widespread selling.

Share: One unit of ownership in a corporation, mutual fund, etc.

Shorting: The act of selling in the market in the anticipation of buying back at a lower price.

Stepping out of your strategy: A very dangerous action for a trader. When you maintain your profitable strategy, you will gain confidence as your profits grow. This confidence will be reinforced every time that you carry out a trade, even in a loss situation because you have come to rely on every level on your strategy being a winner.

Stock: A legal document that indicates the holder's possession of some of the assets of a corporation or other entity.

Stock exchange: The official body of a marketplace where shares of stock are generally bought and sold and the body through which stock is often registered and regulated.

Stockbroker: A person or firm who acts as an agent, on behalf of clients who wish to buy and sell stock.

Stop order: A market order to buy or sell a certain quantity of a certain security if a specified price (the stop price) is reached or passed.

Strategy: Long term action plan for reaching a goal.

The subconscious: Possibly your most important asset when trading. Once your strategy has been fully accepted on a subconscious level, your trading will become more expert; you will no longer be thinking about what has to be done, but will be enjoying the phase that I refer to as 'autonomous ability'.

Tick chart: A chart that shows each price traded in real time as either a dot or a series of dots connected by a line on a chart.

Top: The highest price reached for a given security over a certain time period.

Trade activation: Instructing your broker to perform a transaction on your behalf.

Trade hunting: Hunting for trades often occurs when a trader has a developed strategy, but has not experienced the conditions where the strategy can be used for several days. Frustrated, the trader sets his strategy aside and starts to hunt his charts to see what is going on.

Trading: Buying and selling commodities on a relatively short-term basis.

Trading harmony: Your trading strategy should be aligned with your personal trading ambitions, resources, and understanding of the markets. An example of trading out of harmony would be increasing your contract size without sufficient margin.

Trend: General direction of movement for prices and rates.

Trend lines: Formations created when making a chart illustration - the general direction of movement for prices and rates. Connecting tops or bottoms in the direction of price movement.

Trend pattern: The movement of the market around the trend line; the fluctuations caused by price movement, illustrated on a chart.

Volume: The quantity of shares, bonds or contracts traded during a certain period, for a security or an entire exchange. Also called 'trading volume'. There are distinct types of volume - quoted volume, or the volume of trades, provided by the market, and tick volume, which is a count of the price ticks within a given time period.

Whipsaw effect: Market action that is shown on a chart by erratic and sometimes quite volatile price action. Typically, a certain market direction is apparently established, when the market whipsaws the other way, catching the trader by surprise.

Trading for a bright future